T0268797

MY BOOK OF
Cats
and
Kittens

Project Editor Kritika Gupta
Editors Kathleen Teece, Srijani Ganguly
US Editor Mindy Fichter
US Senior Editor Shannon Beatty
Senior Art Editor Ann Cannings
Art Editor Bhagyashree Nayak
Additional Design Mohd Zishan, Roohi Rais
Illustrator Bettina Myklebust Stovne
Jacket Designer Ann Cannings
DTP Designers Dheeraj Singh, Mohd Rizwan
Senior Picture Researcher Sakshi Saluja
Production Editor Abi Maxwell
Production Controller John Casey
Managing Editors Jonathan Melmoth, Monica Saigal
Managing Art Editors Diane Peyton Jones, Ivy Sengupta
Delhi Creative Heads Glenda Fernandes, Malavika Talukder
Deputy Art Director Mabel Chan
Publishing Director Sarah Larter

Consultant Dr. Bruce Fogle

Content in this title was previously published in
The Everything Book of Cats and Kittens (2018).

First American Edition, 2023
Published in the United States by DK Publishing
1745 Broadway, 20th Floor, New York, NY 10019

A catalog record for this book
is available from the Library of Congress.
ISBN 978-0-7440-7389-8

DK books are available at special discounts when
purchased in bulk for sales promotions, premiums,
fundraising, or educational use. For details, contact:
DK Publishing Special Markets,
1745 Broadway, 20th Floor, New York, NY 10019
SpecialSales@dk.com

Printed and bound in China

For the curious
www.dk.com

MIX
Paper | Supporting
responsible forestry
FSC™ C018179

This book was made with Forest
Stewardship Council™ certified paper –
one small step in DK's commitment to a
sustainable future. For more information
go to www.dk.com/our-green-pledge

Contents

4 Cats

6 World of cats

8 Growing up

10 Colors and markings

12 Short-haired cats

14 American Shorthair

15 British Shorthair

16 Korat

17 Bombay

18 Singapura

19 Abyssinian

20 Egyptian Mau

21 Ocicat

22 Australian Mist

23 Bengal

24 Body language

26 Meowing and talking

28 Chausie

29 Chartreux

30 Toyger

31 Serengeti

32 Siamese

33 Havana

34 American Burmese

35 European Burmese

36 Cornish Rex

37 Devon Rex

38 Training a cat

40 Pixiebob

41 Japanese Bobtail

42 Russian Blue

43 Snowshoe

44 Oriental Shorthair

45 Tonkinese

46 Exotics

48 Super senses

50 Long-haired cats

52 Angora

53 Highlander

54 Ragdoll

55 Maine Coon

56 American Curl

57 Persian

58 Himalayan

59 LaPerm

60 Norwegian Forest Cat

61 Siberian Forest Cat

62 Somali

63 Balinese

64 Looking after cats

66 Feline food

68 Turkish Van

69 Turkish Angora

70 Nebelung

71 Selkirk Rex

72 Tiffanie

73 Chantilly

74 Scottish Fold

75 Manx

76 Birman

77 Aphrodite Giant

78 Mixed-breed cats

80 Hairless cats

82 The cat family

84 Cat characters

86 Cat company

88 Hunting habits

90 All together

92 Glossary

94 Index

96 Acknowledgments

Cat ears have more than twenty muscles.

A cat mostly uses its sensitive nose to smell and touch. It also greets other cats with a nose rub.

A cat's pupils are three times bigger than a human's.

Whiskers are super-sensitive hairs that help a cat judge where things are.

Cats

People have kept cats as pets for thousands of years. They are smaller and gentler than their wild relatives, such as cheetahs and lions. Cats make wonderful companions, whether they are playful and mischievous or prefer snoozing on a human's lap.

The paws of a cat release sweat through the chunky foot pads.

Large to little

Cats vary in size. Smaller cats tend to have a slender body with thin limbs and a thin tail, while bigger cats have a heavier body with thick limbs and a thick tail. Medium-sized cats have a body shape somewhere between these two extremes.

Maine Coon

The Maine Coon is the biggest of all cat breeds. It is around 16 in (40 cm) tall. When compared to the Singapura, the Maine Coon can weigh four times more.

Cat features

Cats are designed to be great hunters. Their excellent balance and super senses help them to climb, jump, run, and pounce. Even domestic cats have wild instincts.

A cat's tail helps it to balance when jumping, or walking along narrow fences.

Sturdy skeleton

A cat skeleton has 230 bones—twenty-four more than a human's. It has a flexible spine and long tail. A cat's tail can have as many as twenty-three bones. Cats have small skulls with jaws that house sharp, pointed teeth.

Cats have strong legs that allow them to jump high.

Every cat releases its own special scent through its foot pads to mark its territory.

Chartreux
The Chartreux is a medium-sized cat. This cat is around 11 in (28 cm) tall. It is smaller than the large Maine Coon but bigger than the tiny Singapura.

Singapura
The Singapura is the smallest of all cats. It is only around 8 in (20 cm) tall. Its ears are large compared to the size of its body.

5

World of cats

Cats first began to live alongside humans in Egypt in around 4,000 BCE. Eventually, people took them by ship to other countries. Now, cats are found on every continent, except for icy Antarctica.

Ancient Egyptians may have given cats as gifts to the Romans.

Snowshoe

This breed was named after its leg markings, which look like snow-white shoes. Its history can be traced back to a litter of kittens born in the 1960s in Philadelphia, Pennsylvania.

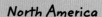

North America

South America

Adopting a cat

Many people choose to adopt cats rather than buy them from breeders, because breeding cats can lead to new breeds with health problems. From former alley cats to Maine Coons—all sorts of furry felines can be adopted from animal shelters.

Brazilian Shorthair

The ancestors of the Brazilian Shorthair came to South America from Europe. They traveled by boat with visiting European sailors in the second century CE.

European Shorthair

The cats that spread to Europe from North Africa are called European Shorthairs. In some countries they are also called Domestic Shorthairs.

Japanese Bobtail

This breed appears in Japanese paintings that are at least a thousand years old. It's easy to spot the Japanese Bobtail because it has a very short tail.

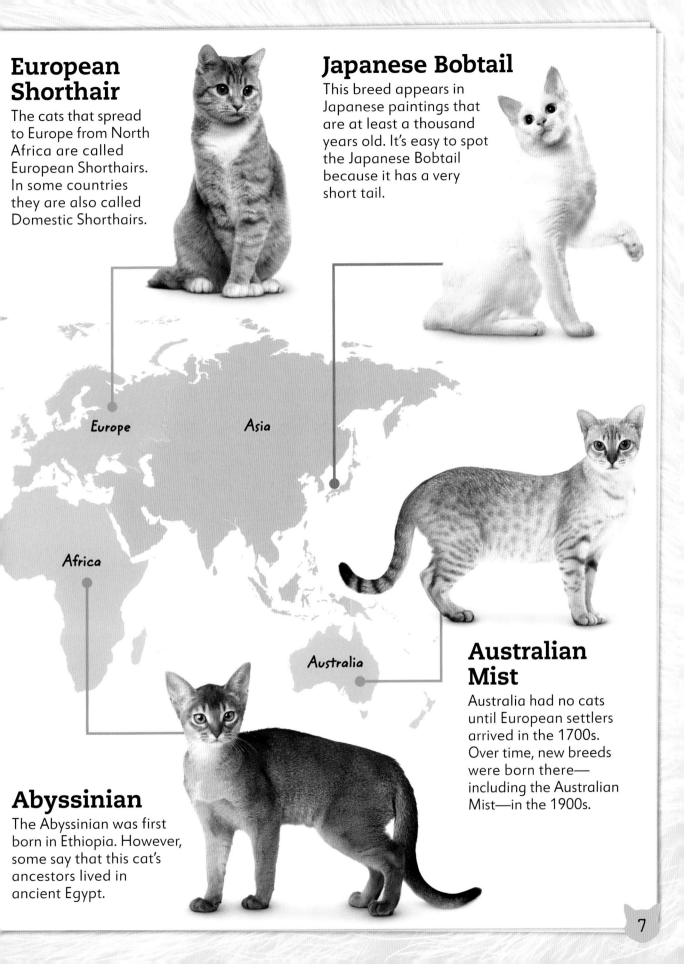

Europe

Asia

Africa

Australia

Australian Mist

Australia had no cats until European settlers arrived in the 1700s. Over time, new breeds were born there—including the Australian Mist—in the 1900s.

Abyssinian

The Abyssinian was first born in Ethiopia. However, some say that this cat's ancestors lived in ancient Egypt.

Growing up

Newborn kittens start out very small, but by six months they are fully grown and have all the skills they need. After birth, kittens stay near their mother to keep warm. They feed on their mother's milk for up to eight weeks before they are fully weaned and ready to eat meat.

Mother cats carry their kittens in their mouths to keep them safe.

One week old
The kitten gains weight and opens its eyes, which are blue in color for the first few weeks. Some breeds keep this eye color, while others develop different colors.

Furry family

A mother cat usually has a litter of three to five kittens, and she can tell them all apart just by the way they smell. She looks after the kittens by feeding, carrying, and cleaning them. Kittens have a lot of brothers and sisters, so growing up together is loads of feline fun!

One day old
The kitten's eyes and ears are closed when it's born. It can't see or hear at this stage. The kitten weighs around 3.5 oz (100 gm), and is so small it can easily fit in the palm of a hand.

Cat birthdays

Cats and humans age differently. A cat grows quickly in the first two years of its life. These two years are equal to the first twenty-five years of a human life. After that, each cat year is equal to four human years. So, if your cat is celebrating its ninth birthday, it is actually fifty-three years old in human terms.

Three weeks old
The ears and eyes are both open by this time. The kitten is able to stand and take its first steps. Its fur is thicker and its body is much bigger.

Life lessons

Kittens are little copycats. They learn by watching and repeating their mother's actions. Playing with the rest of the litter also teaches kittens how to get on with each other.

Kittens playing

Six weeks old
The kitten can now run and jump. It's curious and ready to explore. By this time, the little one has also gotten used to being around humans.

Colors and markings

Cats are covered in hair and their fur comes in many colors with different markings. They usually have three types of hair on their bodies, each with a different job. The topcoat is made up of long guard hairs that keep them dry. The undercoat is made up of stiff awn hairs that protect the cats from grazes, and soft down hairs that keep their body warm.

Named after a striped cloth from Iraq, tabbies have striped fur like tiny tigers.

Tabby

Cats with white coats have no color at all in their fur.

White

Orange

Male cats have brighter orange fur than female ones.

A blue coat is gray with a hint of blue, rather than bright blue.

Blue

Multicolored tortoiseshells, also called torties, have a mix of black, white, and orange fur.

Tortoiseshell

A pointed cat has pale fur with darker parts on the ears, face, paws, and tail.

Pointed

True black cats have fur in one solid color.

Black

Types of fur

Cats of different breeds have varying hair lengths. Some have short fur that is easy to maintain, while others have long, thick fur that requires regular grooming. Some cats have little or no fur at all—they are known as hairless.

Shorthair

Longhair

Hairless

Short-haired cats

Around a hundred years ago, almost all cats had short hair. While there are several long-haired cat breeds now, most domestic cats still have naturally short hair. The coats of short-haired cats are easy to maintain and require less grooming.

The European Shorthair has a dense coat.

Fact file

» **Origin:** Sweden
» **Size:** Medium
» **Weight:** 8–13 lb (3.5–6 kg)
» **Color:** Variety of colors
» **Character:** Social, independent, calm, and affectionate

European Shorthair

Found throughout Europe, this cat is strong and athletic. It is equally comfortable inside and outside the house. Although friendly, the European Shorthair also has an independent streak.

Chinese Li Hua

This loving cat is also known as the Dragon Li. The Chinese Li Hua is hundreds of years old. It is a great hunter and needs a lot of space to run around.

Fact file

» **Origin:** China
» **Size:** Medium
» **Weight:** 9–11 lb (4–5 kg)
» **Color:** Brown mackerel tabby
» **Character:** Friendly, calm, and intelligent

The Chinese Li Hua has a sturdy body.

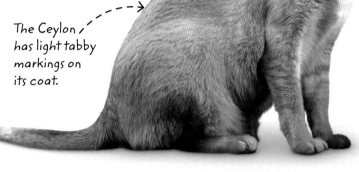

Ceylon

The Ceylon can have yellow or green eyes. It was named after the country of its birth—Ceylon, now called Sri Lanka. This rare breed is very social and playful.

The Ceylon has light tabby markings on its coat.

The Khao Manee can sometimes have different-colored eyes.

Khao Manee

This cat is a beloved native of Thailand, where its name means "white jewel." The Khao Manee was popular with royals in Thailand. Some say it may have even been mentioned in fourteenth century poetry.

The American Wirehair's coat is rough to touch.

American Wirehair

The first cat of this breed was born in 1966 in New York. Each hair of this kitten's wiry coat was bent in the shape of a hook.

American Shorthair

America's oldest cat is bigger but slimmer than its stocky cousin, the British Shorthair. The size of the American Shorthair varies, with some large males being more than twice as big as females.

» **Origin:** United States
» **Size:** Medium to large
» **Weight:** 7–15 lb (3–7 kg)
» **Color:** Variety of colors
» **Character:** Clever, loving, relaxed, and affectionate

> The coat of these cats can grow until they are around four years old.

This breed's short coat thickens in winter for warmth.

The American Shorthair has an athletic body.

Cat communication

The American Shorthair, like other cats, will meow or raise its paws when it wants attention. This breed is very affectionate and enjoys cuddling with its owners.

In 1620, the ancestors of the American Shorthair traveled aboard the Mayflower ship from the UK to the US.

British Shorthair

Often compared to a teddy bear, the British Shorthair has a soft coat and big eyes. One of the most popular cats in Britain, it comes in many colors, including a striking blue.

Fact file

» **Origin:** United Kingdom
» **Size:** Medium to large
» **Weight:** 9–15 lb (4–7 kg)
» **Color:** Variety of colors
» **Character:** Easy-going, affectionate, and friendly

The British Shorthair has a round face.

Blue British Shorthairs have appreared regularly in TV ads for cat food.

This breed has a stocky body with thick fur.

Cheshire Cat

The Cheshire Cat from *Alice's Adventures in Wonderland*, by British writer Lewis Carroll, is a popular feline character. The illustrations of this cat show its coat to have the classic tabby patterns of a British Shorthair.

Its furry tail becomes thinner at the end.

Korat

The Korat is named after the Korat region of northeast Thailand, where it was first discovered. This silver-blue feline is one of the oldest cat breeds. It has a muscular, slim body and a short, dense coat of fur.

» **Origin:** Thailand
» **Size:** Small to medium
» **Weight:** 7–11 lb (3–5 kg)
» **Color:** Silver-blue
» **Character:** Nervous, gentle, affectionate, and alert

Korat kitten

A Korat kitten lacks the silver tipping and the green eye color that the adult cat has. Both of these features take around two years to develop fully.

Its Thai name, *Si-Sawat*, means "grayish-blue."

In the past, a pair of Korats were a popular wedding gift since they were said to bring happiness and fortune.

The Korat has a heart-shaped head with big ears.

This breed has big, bright-green eyes.

It has oval, compact paws.

Bombay

This black beauty is sleek and shiny. Its short, black fur is super-soft to the touch. The Bombay is friendly, fun, and loves to cuddle. This cat looks like a miniature Indian black panther.

Fact file

» **Origin:** United States
» **Size:** Medium
» **Weight:** 6–11 lb (2.5–5 kg)
» **Color:** Black
» **Character:** Loving, playful, friendly, and clever

Look-alike

This cat was named after the Indian city of Bombay (now Mumbai). Mumbai is part of the Western Ghats, which are home to the Bombay's look-alike big cat, the black panther.

The Bombay's muscular body is heavier than it looks.

It has shiny, copper-coloured eyes.

The tip of its nose is slightly rounded.

This breed has sturdy legs with round feet.

The Bombay is closely related to the Burmese cat.

Singapura

The tiny Singapura comes from the island of Singapore. This breed's name is drawn from the Malay word for Singapore, where it is affectionately called the *Kucinta* or "love cat." This friendly cat wants plenty of playtime and company.

» **Origin:** Singapore
» **Size:** Small to medium
» **Weight:** 4–9 lb (2–4 kg)
» **Color:** Mix of brown and cream
» **Character:** Clever, curiou playful, and affectionate

The Singapura's short, fine hair creates bands of brown and cream.

This breed has big eyes compared to its body size.

The Singapura is the smallest domestic cat in the world.

It has small, oval paws.

Singapura cats usually have smaller litters. They only give birth to two or three kittens.

Sepia agouti

The only recognized color for the Singapura is the sepia agouti. It is an ivory coat speckled with brown markings. There are tabby patterns on its face and inner legs. This unique coat is the result of having the Burmese and Abyssinian cats in its ancestry.

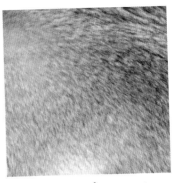

Close-up of the coat

Abyssinian

The Abyssinian is among the oldest cat breeds in the world. It looks like the cats from ancient Egyptian paintings and statues. Although this breed has a quiet personality, it always wants its owner's attention and enjoys the company of other cats.

Fact file

» **Origin:** Ethiopia
» **Size:** Medium
» **Weight:** 4–9 lb (2–4 kg)
» **Color:** Variety of colors
» **Character:** Friendly, content, clever, and active

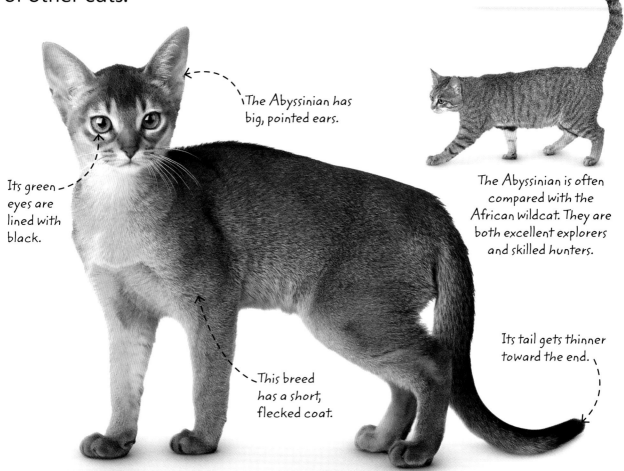

The Abyssinian has big, pointed ears.

Its green eyes are lined with black.

The Abyssinian is often compared with the African wildcat. They are both excellent explorers and skilled hunters.

Its tail gets thinner toward the end.

This breed has a short, flecked coat.

First of its kind

A well-known story states that the founder of the Abyssinian breed may have been a cat named Zula. She was brought to England by an army officer who was in Abyssinia (now Ethiopia) during the 1868 British military campaign in that region.

A painting of Zula

Egyptian Mau

The Egyptian Mau is one of the fastest domestic cats—it can reach a top speed of 30 mph (48 kph). The *Mau*, meaning "cat" in ancient Egyptian, has an eye-catching coat and is an affectionate and playful pet.

» **Origin:** Egypt
» **Size:** Medium
» **Weight:** 7–13 lb (3–6 kg)
» **Color:** Silver, bronze, smoke
» **Character:** Playful, loving, loyal, and active

The Egyptian Mau has big, green eyes.

This breed's short, silky coat is covered in spots and stripes.

It has a loose flap of skin above the hind leg.

Natalie Troubetzkoy, a Russian princess in exile, developed the modern Egyptian Mau cat.

Cats in Egyptian art

Ancient Egyptians believed that cats were like gods. They included cats in various art forms, such as paintings and sculptures. This is a depiction of Ra, the Egyptian sun god, as a spotted and slender cat similar to the Egyptian Mau.

Ocicat

The Ocicat may resemble a wildcat, but it is not closely related to the big cats. It has the friendliness of a pet. A natural athlete, the Ocicat has a graceful frame and a sleek, spotted coat.

» **Origin:** United States
» **Size:** Medium to large
» **Weight:** 7–13 lb (3–6 kg)
» **Color:** Variety of colors
» **Character:** Gentle, loving, curious, and playful

The Ocicat's tail is long and slightly thinner toward the end.

Origin of the Ocicat

The first Ocicat kitten was born to a Siamese and an Abyssinian. It looked very similar to a spotted wildcat called an ocelot, so it was given the name Ocicat.

An ocelot

This breed has large, almond-shaped eyes with dark rims.

The Ocicat comes in twelve accepted fur coat colors.

It has a short, smooth coat with bands of color.

Australian Mist

» **Origin:** Australia and New Zealand
» **Size:** Medium
» **Weight:** 11–15 lb (5–7 kg)
» **Color:** Variety of colors
» **Character:** Energetic, playful, enthusiastic, and friendly

The ancestors of this short-haired cat from Australia hunted mice and rodents in the past. It loves a good chase, but once playtime is over, the Australian Mist enjoys being inside and cuddling.

AUSTRALIA'S NATIONAL CAT

All Australian Mists have green eyes.

It has a short coat that is easy to care for.

The neat, oval paws give this breed a sense of balance.

Born in Australia

The Australian Mist is the first cat breed to have evolved entirely in Australia. It is extremely popular in its native country and has come to be known as a fun, calm, and particularly easy-to-keep pet.

The Australian continent

Bengal

Originally called the Leopardette, the Bengal looks like a mini-leopard with its thick, spotted coat, and large size. It even has a wildcat-like call! But unlike the leopard, this breed loves backyard games, company, and cuddling.

» **Origin:** United States
» **Size:** Large
» **Weight:** 9–18 lb (4–8 kg)
» **Color:** Variety of colors
» **Character:** Confident, clever, active, and affectionate

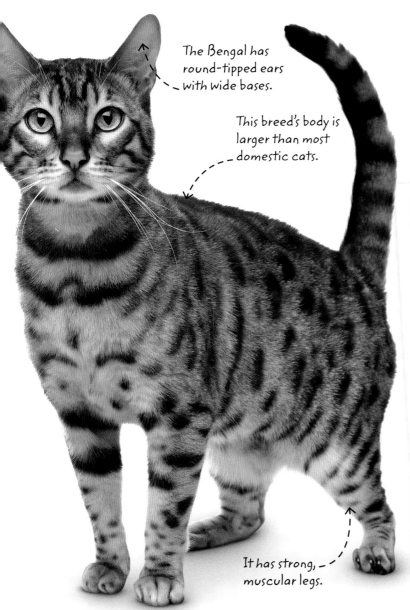

The Bengal has round-tipped ears with wide bases.

This breed's body is larger than most domestic cats.

It has strong, muscular legs.

Bengal cats love water. They might even jump in a tub filled with water!

Stunning coat

While Bengal cats can have many different coat colors, the snow marbled Bengal cat is rare. This cat has blue eyes and a white coat that gives an impression of pearl luster dust on its fur.

Body language

Cats can't use words, but they can show their feelings with their bodies. Learning what their actions mean can help people understand what the cat is trying to communicate.

Only pet cats walk with their tails upright.

Cats rub themselves against their owners to leave their scent on them.

Cats enjoy being petted by people they know.

Telling tails

Cats can lift, lower, and swish their tails. Looking at a cat's tail is often the best way to understand its mood.

Friendly
This cat has its tail held high to show confidence and happiness. Complete satisfaction!

Approach with caution
A scared cat will crouch down low with its tail wrapped underneath its body.

Calm
A low-lying tail means this cat is feeling calm and relaxed, and enjoying its surroundings.

Stay away!
An arched back and tail pointing downward means the cat is angry or scared.

Meowing and talking

Cats can be very vocal for a lot of different reasons. If they are hungry, in need of attention, or trying to complain about something, they will reveal their mood by using specific sounds.

Meow

A hiss is a warning sound that means stay away. A hissing cat is scared and ready to attack.

Hiss

A cat scratching a tree

A meow is the most common sound. A cat meows at its owners when it wants food or attention.

Marking territory

Cats sometimes scratch trees, fences, or posts. This is to clean and sharpen their claws. The scratches are also a way for cats to mark their territory. They usually leave claw marks as high as possible for the most visibility.

A growl is a rumbling noise that suggests the cat is feeling angry and wants to be left alone.

Growl

The cat vocabulary includes at least sixteen different sounds.

Yowl

A yowl is a long, moaning sound. It might mean that the cat is in pain. This should be brought to an adult's attention.

A curious cat will make a birdlike, chirping sound to show interest in something.

Chirp

Purr

When a cat is relaxing or resting, it will often purr to show complete contentment.

Young and old

Kittens make more noises than fully grown cats. They learn early to meow to their mother when they want something. Adult cats meow at people because they see them as their parents.

Young kitten

Adult cat

Chausie

This cat is a creature of habit. It likes to stick to a routine when it comes to sleeping and mealtimes. A newer breed, the Chausie gets its jungle cat looks from its wildcat ancestor.

- » **Origin:** United States
- » **Size:** Large
- » **Weight:** 15–24 lb (7–11 k
- » **Color:** Variety of colors
- » **Character:** Relaxed, affectionate, energetic, and playful

The Chausie has golden eyes sloping toward the outer edge of its ears.

Chausie cats often sit in a way that resembles the position of the statue of the Great Sphinx of Giza in Egypt.

This breed's paws are quite small compared to its size.

It has a rough topcoat over a softer undercoat.

Lock the doors

Chausies have a talent for getting into cupboards. They might walk into the kitchen or the bathroom, and use their paws to open a closed cabinet. In order to stop these curious cats from doing so, many owners install childproof locks on their cabinets and cupboards.

Chartreux

The Chartreux loves the comforts of home and has an undemanding personality. It has a calm and quiet nature, and can be a very affectionate pet. This cat's coat is always blue in color.

Fact file

» **Origin:** France
» **Size:** Medium to large
» **Weight:** 9–13 lb (4–6 kg)
» **Color:** Blue
» **Character:** Confident, clever, loving, and gentle

The Chartreux is known as the national cat of France.

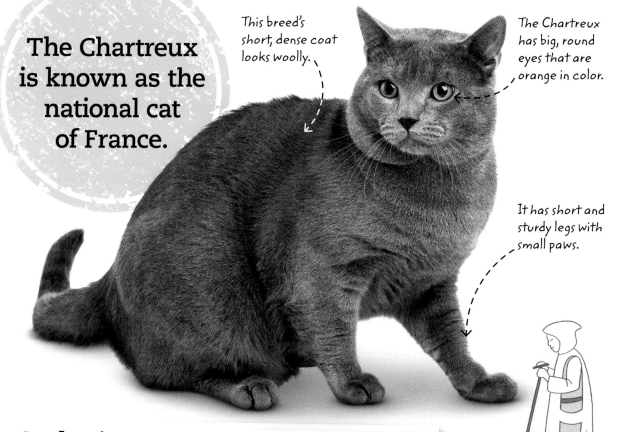

This breed's short, dense coat looks woolly.

The Chartreux has big, round eyes that are orange in color.

It has short and sturdy legs with small paws.

French monks first bred the Chartreux hundreds of years ago to keep mice out of monasteries.

Author's inspiration

The French author Sidonie-Gabrielle Colette, commonly known as Colette, had several Chartreux cats as pets. One of them was named Saha. This beloved pet was the inspiration for a cat in one of her novels.

Colette with her cats

Toyger

Even though the Toyger looks like a smaller version of the mighty tiger, it does not have the wild habits of big cats. The striking, tigerlike stripes on its body give this pet cat a unique look.

» **Origin:** United States
» **Size:** Medium to large
» **Weight:** 12–22 lb (5.5–10 kg)
» **Color:** Brown, tiger-striped tabby
» **Character:** Intelligent, affectionate, energetic, and playful

The Toyger is sometimes also called a "toy tiger."

The Toyger has an M-shaped pattern on its forehead.

This breed has a brown tabby coat.

Its tail is long and muscular.

The Toyger has big, strong legs.

Cover model

In 2007, an issue of *LIFE* magazine featured the Toyger breed for its cover story. The cat on the cover was an eleven-month-old Toyger named Sumatra.

LIFE
AMERICA'S WEEKEND MAGAZINE
It's a tiger...
It's a house cat...
Meet the Toyger
— AMERICA'S NEXT SUPERPET
23

Serengeti

The gentle and outgoing Serengeti forms deep connections with its owners and will follow them anywhere. Expect all kinds of action and adventure from this eager explorer.

Fact file

» **Origin:** United States
» **Size:** Medium
» **Weight:** 9–15 lb (4–7 kg)
» **Color:** Spotted pattern on golden, gray, or black fur
» **Character:** Friendly, confident, active, and alert

The Serengeti is known for being a very talkative cat breed.

Connection to Africa

The Serengeti might look like a wild serval cat, but it comes from two domestic breeds—the Bengal and Oriental. It is named after a part of Africa where wildcats live, even though the first Serengeti was born in California.

Serengeti, Africa

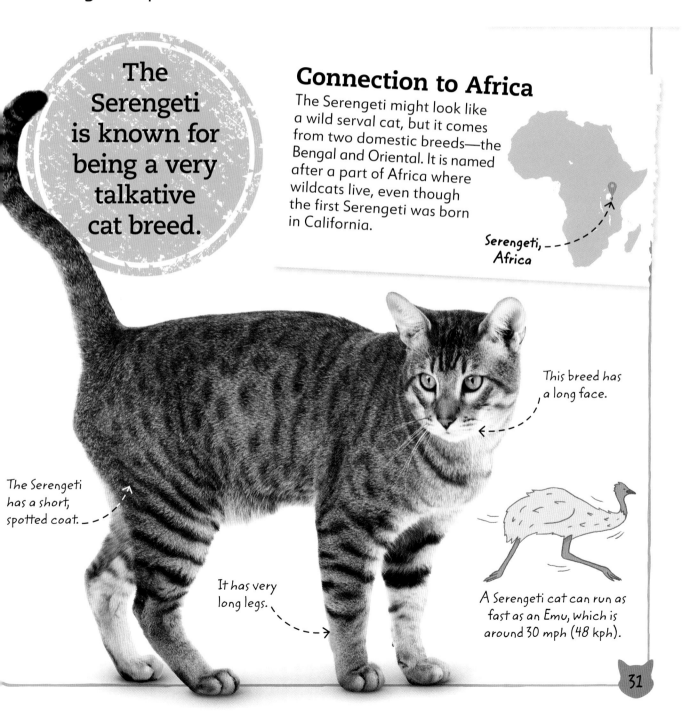

This breed has a long face.

The Serengeti has a short, spotted coat.

It has very long legs.

A Serengeti cat can run as fast as an Emu, which is around 30 mph (48 kph).

31

Siamese

Siamese cats came from the Royal Courts of Siam, now known as Thailand. As well as their name, these cats have kept their majestic looks and graceful manner. They enjoy company and conversation.

- » **Origin:** Thailand
- » **Size:** Medium
- » **Weight:** 4–11 lb (2–5 kg)
- » **Color:** Pointed, meaning pale bodies with darker faces, legs, and tails
- » **Character:** Clever, lively, friendly, and noisy

This breed's short, silky coat is mostly cream, but dark on the ears, face, paws, and tail.

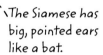

The Siamese has big, pointed ears like a bat.

Its almond-shaped eyes are blue in color.

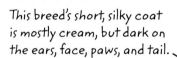

All Siamese kittens are born pure white. The darker colors appear gradually as they grow older.

In Thailand, this cat is called *wichien-maat*, meaning "moon diamond."

Ancient muse

The history of the Siamese includes mostly myths and legends rather than facts. The true tale of this cat is now lost to time. But ancient paintings and statues showing a cat similar to a Siamese suggest that this cat may have been around for thousands of years.

Havana

The Havana has been nicknamed the "chocolate delight" because of its beautiful brown coat and affectionate nature. This cat loves being around people and often demands attention when feeling ignored.

- » **Origin:** United Kingdom and United States
- » **Size:** Medium to large
- » **Weight:** 6–10 lb (2.5–4.5 kg)
- » **Color:** Rich brown, lilac
- » **Character:** Gentle, calm, smart, and curious

Its coat is of a single color with no other markings.

The Havana has oval-shaped, green eyes.

This breed has straight, slim legs with oval feet.

The Havana loves the company of other cats and dogs.

Bulblike muzzle

The Havana's rounded muzzle sticks out from its head. It is an unusual look, which has led people to describe its muzzle as being like the end of a light bulb.

American Burmese

The Burmese breeds are often called "bricks wrapped in silk." This is because they are much heavier than they look, and their glossy fur is super-soft to the touch. These cats love to hang out with humans.

» **Origin:** Myanmar (formerly Burma)
» **Size:** Medium
» **Weight:** 7–11 lb (3–5 kg)
» **Color:** Brown, gray
» **Character:** Friendly, playful, confident, and affectionate

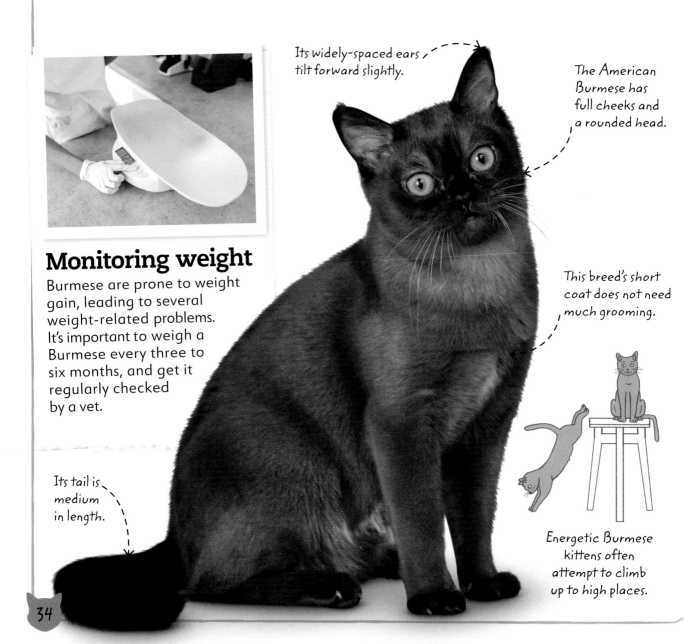

Monitoring weight

Burmese are prone to weight gain, leading to several weight-related problems. It's important to weigh a Burmese every three to six months, and get it regularly checked by a vet.

Its widely-spaced ears tilt forward slightly.

The American Burmese has full cheeks and a rounded head.

This breed's short coat does not need much grooming.

Its tail is medium in length.

Energetic Burmese kittens often attempt to climb up to high places.

European Burmese

The European Burmese is very similar to the American breed in both looks and personality, but it comes in different colors. This cat loves companionship and needs a lot of affection.

Fact file

» **Origin:** Myanmar (formerly Burma)
» **Size:** Medium
» **Weight:** 7–11 lb (3–5 kg)
» **Color:** Variety of colors
» **Character:** Affectionate, curious, and loyal

Influencing others

Burmese cats are extroverts and love to socialize. These friendly traits may also be seen in felines that have a Burmese for a parent. Burmese Bombay and Burmilla are two such breeds.

A Burmilla cat

The European Burmese has a tail with a rounded tip.

Ancestors of the Burmese cats lived in temples across Myanmar, many hundreds of years ago.

This breed's back legs are longer than the front legs.

Cornish Rex

The Cornish Rex is known for its covering of curls. This cat is often compared to dogs since it enjoys playing fetch, running around, and following family members.

The Cornish Rex has very big ears that sit high on the head.

The first curly-haired kitten was born in 1950 in Cornwall, UK.

The short, fine coat of this cat lies in neat waves.

Its slim body is packed with muscles.

Greyhound dog

Greyhound cat

The Cornish Rex is sometimes called the "Greyhound" of the cat world. This is because it has long legs and a tucked-up torso, which makes it look like a Greyhound.

Some Cornish Rex kittens lose their wavy coats for a few weeks and have a temporary, suede-like coat.

Devon Rex

Another type of curly-haired kitten was born ten years after the Cornish Rex, in the neighboring English county of Devon. The Devon Rex has a pixie face, bat ears, long neck, and of course, a curly coat.

Fact file

» **Origin:** United Kingdom
» **Size:** Medium
» **Weight:** 7–9 lb (3–4 kg)
» **Color:** Variety of colors
» **Character:** Affectionate, energetic, playful, and curious

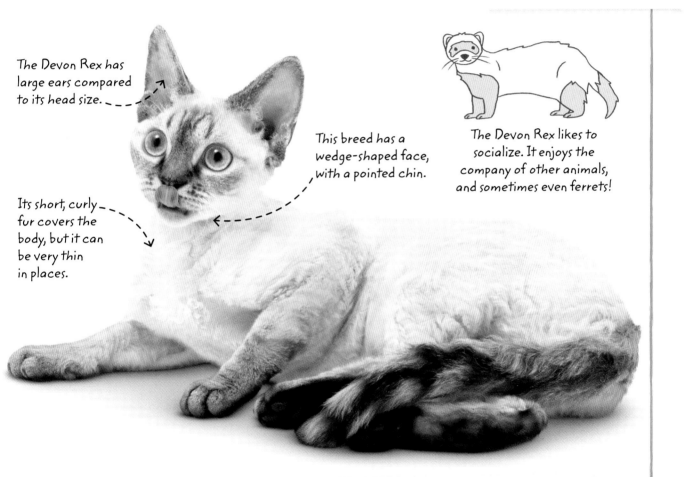

The Devon Rex has large ears compared to its head size.

This breed has a wedge-shaped face, with a pointed chin.

The Devon Rex likes to socialize. It enjoys the company of other animals, and sometimes even ferrets!

Its short, curly fur covers the body, but it can be very thin in places.

Origins of Devon Rex

These cats first appreared in Devon in the late 1950s. A woman named Miss Cox found that a stray cat in her care had given birth to an odd-looking, curly-haired kitten. Charmed by its tiny features and wavy curls, she named it Kirlee.

County of Devon, United Kingdom

Training a cat

While it may sound unusual, cats can be trained to perform basic tricks. Most felines are willing to learn quite a few commands if they are rewarded with treats. Training a cat makes it easier to control and manage its behavior.

Some cats can be trained to go on walks with a leash.

Basic tricks

Cats are very independent, so they will need to be encouraged to learn tricks. Tasty treats and a lot of praise will make them more likely to perform.

The cat should be given a treat if it meows when its name is called out. Over time, the feline will develop the habit of meowing in response to its name. This command can help if the cat gets lost outsic or trapped somewhere.

Cats need a harness with their leash since they can easily slip out of a collar.

A cat will only be open to learning tricks, such as waving a paw, if the training is enjoyable. It should never be forced to learn tricks. If there are signs that the cat is unhappy, such as hissing, the training should be stopped.

A cat will naturally wait and watch if a treat is held over its head. To teach a cat to sit on command, the owner can try saying "sit" while the treat is being held or moved around overhead.

Pixiebob

This fabulous feline looks like a wild bobcat but acts like a pet dog. The Pixiebob enjoys playing fetch and other games. Many Pixiebobs like going for walks!

- » **Origin:** United States
- » **Size:** Medium to large
- » **Weight:** 9–18 lb (4–8 kg)
- » **Color:** Brown with black stripes
- » **Character:** Energetic, friendly, bold, and clever

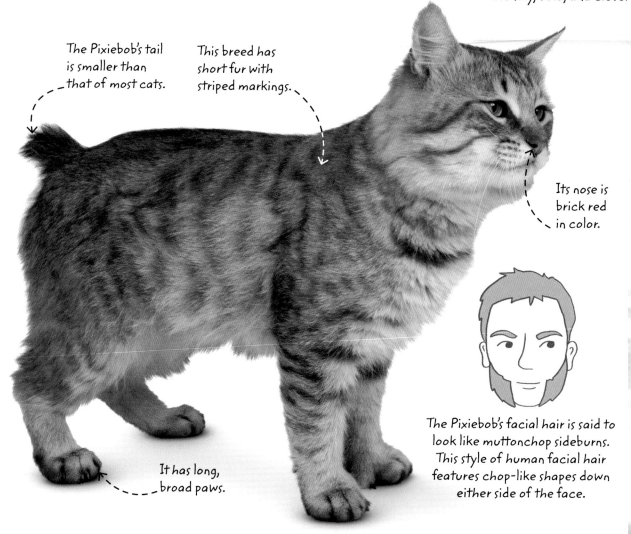

The Pixiebob's tail is smaller than that of most cats.

This breed has short fur with striped markings.

Its nose is brick red in color.

It has long, broad paws.

The Pixiebob's facial hair is said to look like muttonchop sideburns. This style of human facial hair features chop-like shapes down either side of the face.

Extra toes

Cats are usually born with five toes on their front paws and four toes on the back paws. This is not the case with all Pixiebobs. Some of them can have as many as seven toes on each paw!

A Pixiebob's paw with an extra toe

Japanese Bobtail

This cat might almost be mistaken for a rabbit! It has a tiny tail, unlike most other cats. The Japanese Bobtail loves to talk and cuddle.

- » **Origin:** Japan
- » **Size:** Medium
- » **Weight:** 7–11 lb (3–5 kg)
- » **Color:** Variety of colors
- » **Character:** Reliable, clever, playful, and affectionate

The Japanese Bobtail's ears are set wide apart.

These cats are called "singing cats" because of their musical meows.

Lucky charm

Maneki-neko (beckoning cat) is used as a lucky charm all over Japan. This ceramic cat looks like the Japanese Bobtail, and has one paw raised in the air.

This breed has a muscular but slender body.

It has a soft, silky coat.

In the past, these cats were used to protect silkworms from rodents. Silkworms were valuable since they produced silk.

Russian Blue

The Russian Blue is known for its blue-gray coat and bright green eyes. This beautiful breed is believed to have originated in the Russian city of Archangel, close to the Arctic Circle. It is considered lucky in Russia.

» **Origin:** Russia
» **Size:** Medium
» **Weight:** 8–11 lb (3.5–5 kg)
» **Color:** Various shades of blue
» **Character:** Shy, agile, quiet, and affectionate

The Russian Blue's wide-set ears are very thin at the tips.

Its plush, dense coat stands out from the body.

The topcoat of this cat has silver-tipped hair.

Czar Nicholas I had a pet Russian Blue cat named Vashka.

This breed has long and powerful back legs.

Changing eye color

Like most kittens, Russian Blues are born with blue eyes. Over time, as the kitten gets older, the blue fades to a light yellow, then turns to yellow with a green ring, and finally becomes a bright green.

A Russian Blue kitten

Snowshoe

Named after its pure white paws, the sweet Snowshoe cat loves to stay inside. This intelligent and responsive cat enjoys spending time with its family. Its calm personality makes it a good choice for first-time cat owners.

The Snowshoe's ears have rounded tips.

The first Snowshoe kittens were born to a Siamese cat in the 1960s.

This breed has long, white mittens on its paws.

Internet celebrity

A mixed-breed cat with a possible Snowshoe parent became famous in 2012 for her sour expressions. Originally named Tardar Sauce, she earned the nickname "Grumpy Cat."

Snowshoe cats always have blue eyes.

Oriental Shorthair

This confident cat can be very alert. The Oriental Shorthair expects a lot of play and entertainment. Its coat can have hundreds of colors and patterns.

» **Origin:** Thailand
» **Size:** Medium
» **Weight:** 8–13 lb (3.5–6 k
» **Color:** Variety of colors
» **Character:** Clever, playful, loyal, and affectionate

Smoky bands
Smoke-patterned Oriental Shorthairs have two bands of colors. The top layer can be blue, black, red, chocolate, or tortoiseshell. The shorter hair underneath it is always white or very pale. This layer can be seen whenever the cat moves around.

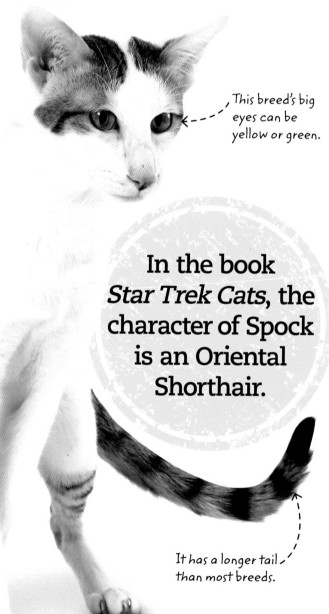

This breed's big eyes can be yellow or green.

In the book *Star Trek Cats*, the character of Spock is an Oriental Shorthair.

It has a longer tail than most breeds.

The Oriental Shorthair has small, oval paws.

44

Tonkinese

Active and friendly, the Tonkinese gets along with children as well as other pets. This cat has the Burmese and Siamese for parents. It was the first breed to be born with aqua-colored eyes.

Fact file

» **Origin:** United States
» **Size:** Medium
» **Weight:** 6–12 lb (2.5–5.5 kg)
» **Color:** Variety of colors
» **Character:** Friendly, active, and clever

People pleaser

This breed is very playful and outgoing. It enjoys spending time with people, and loves to interact and play with them. The Tonkinese, nicknamed the "Tonk", likes riding on its owner's shoulders or sitting on their lap.

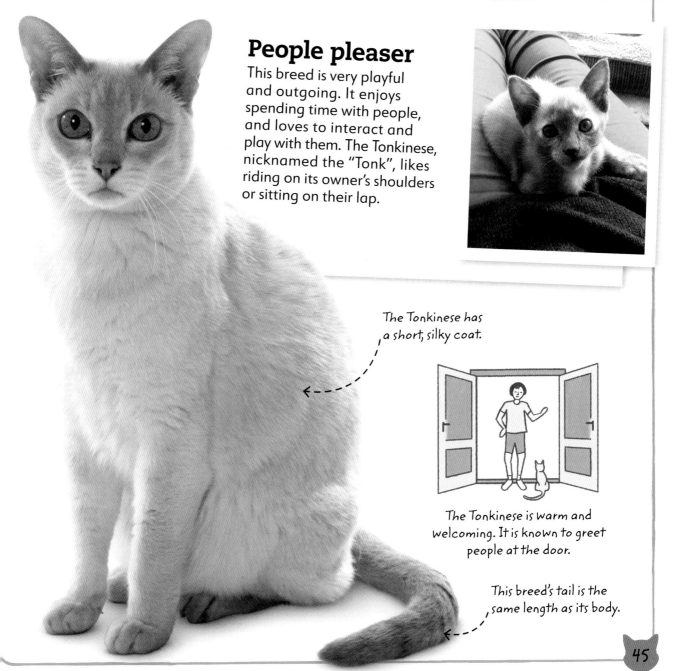

The Tonkinese has a short, silky coat.

The Tonkinese is warm and welcoming. It is known to greet people at the door.

This breed's tail is the same length as its body.

Exotics

These cats look and behave like the long-haired Persian, but the fur is much easier to manage. Exotics can be of different colors and have a gentle personality.

The dense, plush coat is made of hairs that stick out from the cat's body.

The eyes of Exotics can be of various colors depending on the coat color.

They have medium- to large-sized bodies.

Personality

Exotics are easygoing and affectionate cats. They are sweet and curious. These lively felines love attention and cuddling.

Exotics are gentle cats. They get along well with children and other pets, such as dogs, because of their even-tempered nature.

While they may look like Persians, Exotics are much more active. These cats love playtime and will chase balls around the house.

Long-haired Exotics

Exotics can also have long hair. Long-haired kittens can sometimes be born in the same litter as Exotic shorthairs.

Super senses

Cat senses are much more developed than those of humans. This is why they like nighttime, when they can see, hear, and smell without being seen. Cats have a great sense of direction. There are many stories about them finding their way home over long distances.

Cats are so sensitive to vibrations in the air that some can sense earthquakes even before humans.

Hearing

Cats can hear low-pitched sounds just as well as humans, but are much better at hearing high-pitched noises. Their pointed, triangle-shaped ears can move in the direction of the tiniest sound.

Touch

Cats have sensitive, long whiskers that help them judge the width of spaces. They also have sensory hair on their body and legs, which helps them to climb as well as measure distances.

Cat pupils in bright light

Cat pupils in dimmer light

Cat eyes

Cats can see as well at night as in daytime. A cat's dark pupils narrow to black slits during the day when there's a lot of light. At night, the pupils get bigger to allow more light to enter the eyes.

Finding a way

According to a popular story, when Henry Wriothesley, a British earl, was imprisoned in the Tower of London in 1601, his pet cat found its way to him. It is said that the cat walked all the way across London to the Tower, crossing roofs until it found the earl.

A portrait of Henry with his cat

Sight

Cats have excellent vision. Their eyes have a reflective layer that bounces almost all light to the back of the eye. This makes it easy for them to see in the dark, and causes their eyes to glow with reflected light at night.

Smell and taste

When cats come across something unknown, they smell it. Their sense of smell helps them recognize objects, other animals, humans, and food. Their sense of taste is different from humans, since they can't taste sweet things.

49

Long-haired cats

The first known long-haired cats lived in Central Asia many centuries ago. These breeds have long, thick, and fluffy fur that requires regular grooming to keep it tangle-free and soft.

The British Longhair has dense fur.

Fact file

- » **Origin:** United Kingdom
- » **Size:** Medium
- » **Weight:** 9–15 lb (4–7 kg)
- » **Color:** Variety of colors
- » **Character:** Calm, patient, clever, and affectionate

British Longhair

Known as the Lowlander in the United States, this cat is the cousin of the British Shorthair. It makes an excellent pet because of its easygoing nature.

Much like human fingerprints, no two American Bobtail tails are the same.

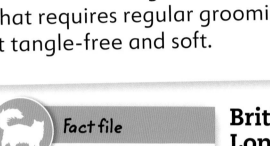

The tufted ears of an American Bobtail have a slightly rounded tip.

American Bobtail

The American Bobtail has a very short tail. This cat is intelligent, and is known to be sensitive to human emotions.

Fact file

- » **Origin:** United States
- » **Size:** Medium
- » **Weight:** 7–15 lb (3–7 kg)
- » **Color:** Variety of colors
- » **Character:** Alert, active, affectionate, and playful

Ural Rex

The Ural Rex is possibly one of the oldest cats of the rex breeds. This rare cat may have lived in the Ural region of Russia since the late 1940s.

Fact file

- » **Origin:** Russia
- » **Size:** Small to medium
- » **Weight:** 8–13 lb (3.5–6 kg)
- » **Color:** Variety of colors
- » **Character:** Calm, quiet, and easygoing

The Ural Rex has a medium-long coat that falls in waves.

Fact file

- » **Origin:** Kuril Islands
- » **Size:** Small to medium
- » **Weight:** 7–10 lb (3–4.5 kg)
- » **Color:** Variety of colors
- » **Character:** Active, friendly, and curious

Kurilian Bobtail

A long, thick coat protects this breed from the harsh winters of the Kuril Islands, off Japan, where it is from. This cat has a sturdy build and strong legs.

The Kurilian Bobtail's tail is a soft ball of long hair, carried high.

Neva Masquerade

This cat is named after the Neva River in Saint Petersburg, Russia, where it was first born. This breed is known for becoming particularly attached to children.

The thick coat of the Neva Masquerade is weatherproof.

Fact file

- » **Origin:** Russia
- » **Size:** Medium to large
- » **Weight:** 9–15 lb (4–7 kg)
- » **Color:** Variety of colors
- » **Character:** Friendly, gentle, and affectionate

Angora

The Angora was the first long-haired cat breed in Europe. Its silky coat can be a variety of colors. This cat loves to be the center of attention and often forms a close bond with its owner.

Fact file

» **Origin:** United Kingdom
» **Size:** Medium
» **Weight:** 4–9 lb (2–4 kg)
» **Color:** Variety of colors
» **Character:** Confident, playful, clever, and affectionate

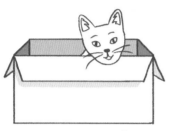

Like most cats, the Angora can spend hours playing with an empty cardboard box.

The Angora is also known as the Oriental Longhair.

The Angora has a triangular head.

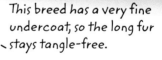

This breed has a very fine undercoat, so the long fur stays tangle-free.

1813 portrait by Louis Léopold Boilly

The painted feline

The modern-day Angora looks very similar to long-haired cats in nineteenth century paintings. A portrait by the French painter Louis Léopold Boilly shows one such cat sitting in the lap of a child.

Highlander

This long-haired cat has a thick, shaggy coat and curled ears. Even though it might look like a wildcat, the Highlander is gentle, and it gets along well with children.

Fact file

» **Origin:** United States
» **Size:** Large
» **Weight:** 10–18 lb (4.5–8 kg)
» **Color:** Variety of colors
» **Character:** Friendly, gentle, affectionate, and playful

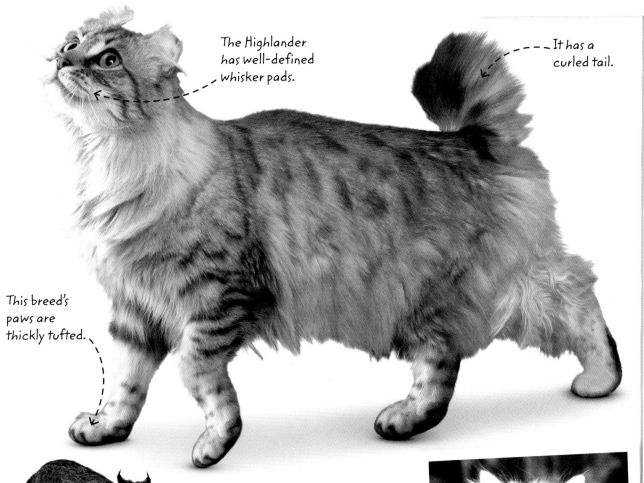

The Highlander has well-defined whisker pads.

It has a curled tail.

This breed's paws are thickly tufted.

The Highlander cat looks like a small lynx, even though it doesn't have a wildcat for a parent.

Straight ears

Highlander kittens have straight ears when they are born. As the cats grow older, their ears start to curl back but do not curl more than ninety degrees.

A Highlander kitten

Ragdoll

Despite being bigger than the average cat, the relaxed Ragdoll is content to just hang out rather than use up a lot of energy. This cat loves having its silky, soft fur stroked and brushed.

» **Origin:** United States
» **Size:** Large
» **Weight:** 10—16 lb (4.5—7.5 kg)
» **Color:** Variety of colors
» **Character:** Calm, gentle, loving, and affectionate

This cat tends to become so relaxed in its owner's arms that it goes limp, like a ragdoll. This is how it got its name!

This breed has a large body with big bones.

The Ragdoll has bright-blue eyes.

Its woolly undercoat is covered with a long, silky overcoat.

Emotional support cats

Ragdoll cats are gentle, and love being carried and petted for long periods. Their affectionate nature makes them an excellent choice for support-animal roles. This means they help children and adults who get sad or anxious to feel better.

Maine Coon

Regarded as the United States's native cat, this breed is named after the US state of Maine where it was first born. The Maine Coon is the biggest domestic cat. It is often called a gentle giant because of its super size and loving personality.

» **Origin:** United States
» **Size:** Large
» **Weight:** 10–20 lb
   (4.5–9 kg)
» **Color:** Variety of colors
» **Character:** Bold, clever,
   affectionate, and loyal

Tall tales

During the French Revolution, the Queen of France, Marie Antoinette, was said to have sent her pet cats to the United States for safety. The story went that one of these was a parent of the first Maine Coon.

Marie Antoinette

—The Maine Coon has a fluffy ruff around its neck.

— This breed's coat has patterns and markings similar to a raccoon.

A Maine Coon played the role of Mrs. Norris in the *Harry Potter*™ films.

Its enormous, bushy tail is at least as long as the body.

American Curl

This breed is named after its unusual ears, which curl backward. Although it has a soft voice, the American Curl is not shy about demanding attention. Its friendly and loving nature makes it perfect for families.

» **Origin:** United States
» **Size:** Medium
» **Weight:** 7–11 lb (3–5 kg)
» **Color:** Variety of colors
» **Character:** Alert, intelligent, affectionate, and gentle

Forever kitten

The popular character Peter Pan never grew up. The American Curl is sometimes called the "Peter Pan of cats" because of its playful, kitten-like personality.

The American Curl has walnut-shaped eyes.

This breed comes from a single litter of kittens with curled ears.

This breed has a silky coat.

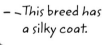

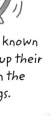

It has a thick, fluffy tail.

These cats are known to gently wake up their owners when the alarm rings.

Persian

The fluffy Persian is one of the oldest cat breeds. This puffball is instantly recognizable for its flowing fur. It likes to stay at home, getting a lot of fuss and attention.

» **Origin:** Iran (formerly Persia)
» **Size:** Medium to large
» **Weight:** 9–13 lb (4–6 kg)
» **Color:** Variety of colors
» **Character:** Gentle, playful, affectionate, and sweet

A dollface Persian cat

Dollface

Persians either have a "doll" or a "peke" face. Dollface Persians have longer noses, and are more similar to the first cats of this breed. Peke-face Persians have flatter faces, like Pekingese dogs—the animal they were named after.

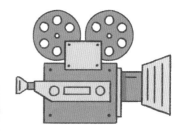

Persian cats have starred in movies and cartoons. It's commonly believed that Garfield™, the popular cartoon cat, is an orange Persian tabby.

It has thick fur that may easily become knotted and tangled.

This Persian has a peke face.

This breed has a fluffy tail.

Himalayan

The Himalayan descends from Persian and Siamese cats. This blue-eyed beauty likes a lot of love in quiet surroundings. Be warned though—it needs a lot of brushing to stop its coat from tangling.

» **Origin:** United States and United Kingdom
» **Size:** Medium to large
» **Weight:** 7–13 lb (3–6 kg)
» **Color:** Variety of colors
» **Character:** Calm, relaxed, affectionate, and sweet

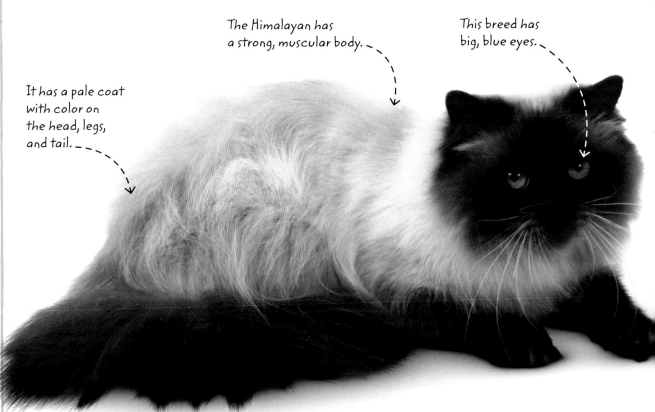

The Himalayan has a strong, muscular body.

This breed has big, blue eyes.

It has a pale coat with color on the head, legs, and tail.

Himalayan rabbit

The Himalayan cat is named after the Himalayan rabbit. This is because both animals have similar patterns on their fur.

A Himalayan rabbit

The Himalayan's flattened nose can make it look similar to a Pug dog.

LaPerm

Tumbling curls are the LaPerm's trademark, but it is also known for its playful personality. Like curious kittens, the LaPerm loves to be in the thick of the action.

Fact file

» **Origin:** United States and United Kingdom
» **Size:** Small to medium
» **Weight:** 6–9 lb (2.5–4 kg)
» **Color:** Variety of colors
» **Character:** Active, affectionate, friendly, and playful

The LaPerm has large, tufted ears.

Its coat of loose curls is soft to the touch.

This breed's body is heavy for its medium size.

Curls and whiskers

The tightest ringlets on this cat's coat appear on its neck, ruff, and along the tail. The LaPerm is also known for having very long whiskers.

Kittens of this long-haired cat are sometimes born bald.

Norwegian Forest Cat

Fact file

» **Origin:** Norway
» **Size:** Large
» **Weight:** 9–20 lb (4–9 kg
» **Color:** Variety of colors
» **Character:** Clever, friendly, alert, and gentle

A native of Norway, where it is called *Skogkatt*, meaning "forest cat," this breed is very popular in Scandinavia. It is a skilled climber, with a fur coat fully equipped for the coldest winters.

Its thick, waterproof coat covers a warm, woolly undercoat.

This breed has strong claws for gripping and climbing.

A Viking ship

Viking shipmates

There are several legends about the origins of the Norwegian Forest Cat. One such tale is that the ancestors of this cat might have sailed with the Vikings, to hunt mice on their ships.

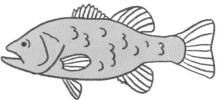

Norwegian Forest Cats are good hunters, and are even known to sometimes catch fish.

Siberian Forest Cat

Fact file

» **Origin:** Russia
» **Size:** Medium to large
» **Weight:** 8–18 lb (3.5–8 kg)
» **Color:** Variety of colors
» **Character:** Affectionate, athletic, and playful

This furry cat has a very thick coat, which kept it warm in its original home in the frozen forests of Russia. The Siberian Forest Cat's coat grows slowly and may take five years or more to fully grow.

This breed has round eyes, usually gold or green.

The first known writing about a Siberian cat was from 1,000 CE.

Its large, round paws balance the body weight.

Heroic mousers

After World War II, two hundred Siberian Forest Cats were sent from Tyumen to Leningrad (now Saint Petersburg), Russia, to its keep galleries and museums free from rodents. Tyumen has a park with twelve feline statues, honoring these cats.

The Siberian Cat Park in Tyumen, Russia

Siberian cats are featured widely in Russian fairy tales.

Somali

Somali cats love climbing trees or hanging out on top of tall furniture. These curious cats always have their eyes on the next adventure. The earliest Somali cats were super-furry versions of the Abyssinian breed.

Fact file

» **Origin:** United States and Australia
» **Size:** Medium
» **Weight:** 6–12 lb (2.5–5.5 kg)
» **Color:** Variety of colors
» **Character:** Gentle, playf clever, and lively

Winter coat

Somalis grow a majestic full coat on their bodies and a ruff around their necks in the winter months. Even though it is not enough to fully protect them from the cold, these cats love to go out in the snow.

The Somali's eyes have a dark rim.

The Somali has a bushy tail, which looks a lot like a fox's tail.

This breed has a lean but strong body.

Its legs match the color of its body.

Balinese

Balinese cats are the same as Siamese cats, but with long hair. These cats are quiet, but still like a lot of attention. They are full of energy and can often be found exploring or making mischief.

- » **Origin:** United States
- » **Size:** Medium
- » **Weight:** 6–11 lb (2.5–5 kg)
- » **Color:** Pointed, with darker face, legs, and tail
- » **Character:** Loving, curious, active, and friendly

Elegant felines

Known for their elegance, Balinese cats were named after Balinese temple dancers. These graceful dancers, from the Asian island of Bali, are famous for their soft, delicate dance movements.

A Balinese temple dancer

This cat loves examining vacuum cleaners and looking inside bags.

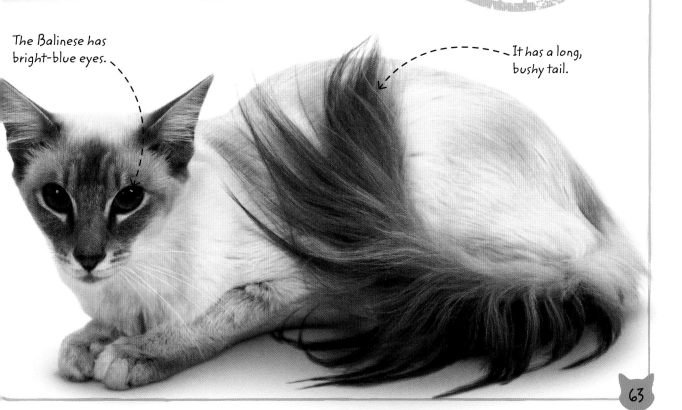

The Balinese has bright-blue eyes.

It has a long, bushy tail.

Cats should be made familiar with carriers at home before they are taken on a trip.

Grooming

Grooming a cat is very important to keep it healthy. Its nails should be trimmed by a groomer or an adult to avoid scratching. Brushing keeps the fur clean and tangle-free. Long-haired cats may also need baths, and a trip to the groomer to have their fur trimmed.

Safe transport

Cats travel well if trained young. When traveling in a car or any other kind of vehicle, cats should be safely kept inside travel carriers.

Looking after cats

Bringing a new pet home for the first time is very exciting, but taking care of it is a big responsibility. Everything a cat needs should be kept ready before bringing it home. Things that may be harmful for the cat should be put away.

Food and water

Cats can be fed a mix of wet food with some dry food and fresh food. It is best to leave out both a bowl of food and a bowl of water for them.

Cat naps

Cats are most active and alert in the evening or early morning. They sleep for long hours during the day, so a blanket-lined basket or a soft cat bed is ideal for them.

Kittens can be taught to use the litter box when they turn four weeks old.

House rules

Here are some points to keep in mind when taking care of a cat.

 The water bowl should always be full.

 Serve food at the same time each day to follow a routine.

 The cat needs to be given a lot of love, but should be left alone when it has had enough.

 Regular times can be set aside for play.

 A cat door should be installed to allow the cat to come and go.

 The cat's fur needs to be brushed to keep it clean.

 Bad behavior, such as scratching furniture, should be firmly stopped.

Toilet time

Cats go to the bathroom in a litter box, which needs to be emptied daily. There are two kinds of litter boxes: open and covered. The litter itself can be a variety of materials, such as clay or corn.

Scratch and play

Cats love to scratch things! They have to be trained not to scratch furniture. Having a scratching post in the house helps. Playing with colorful toys and eye-catching objects is something else cats enjoy.

Scratching post with toy attached

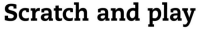

65

Feline food

A healthy diet is important for cats. They are carnivores, which means they eat meat. This can be given in the form of fresh, wet, or dry food, with plenty of water. Cats should be given different flavors of food to see which they enjoy the most.

A balanced diet

A balanced diet includes wet food, fresh meat, and dry food. Wet food helps kittens move on from milk, and older cats to take in more water. Dry food is important since it keeps their teeth healthy and clean.

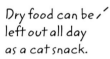

Dry food can be left out all day as a cat snack.

Changing appetite

Adult cats have one big, main meal a day. However, the menu should be changed regularly to keep the cat's interest. Kittens, on the other hand, have smaller tummies, so they eat smaller meals, but more often.

A kitten eating solid food

Some cats prefer dry food over fresh or wet food.

Foods to avoid

Certain food should not be given to cats. Cow's milk might give some cats an upset tummy. Bad raw fish can make them ill, and dark chocolate can be dangerous for them.

Cats love fresh meat, but it should be cooked properly before serving.

Milk, raw fish, and chocolate

Water

Cats should drink a lot of clean water every day. This keeps their bodies healthy and helps them to digest food. A cat can become sick if it doesn't get enough water.

Some cats like drinking water from a bowl, while others enjoy a sip from running water.

A cat's tongue

A cat has small, backward-facing, curved spines on its tongue. These tiny spines, called papillae, feel like sandpaper. They help the cat to eat and drink as well as to groom and cool itself. Papillae are made of keratin—the same substance that makes up human skin.

A close-up of a cat's tongue

Turkish Van

This cat comes from the Lake Van region of Turkey, where it is thought to bring good luck. Also called the "swimming cat," the Turkish Van loves being in water. When this energetic and loving cat gets upset, its pink nose turns red.

» **Origin:** Turkey
» **Size:** Medium to large
» **Weight:** 9–15 lb (4–7 kg)
» **Color:** White body with a colored head and tail
» **Character:** Active, sma[ll] playful, and independen[t]

Its coat of silky white fur is easy to comb.

Turkish Vans can have a naughty streak, and are known to steal glasses.

This breed can have colored spots on its ears.

Turkish Vankedisi

The Turkish Vankedisi is the all-white cousin of the Turkish Van. This breed looks and behaves like the Turkish Van, but it does not have any color markings on its head or tail.

Turkish Angora

This ancient breed is considered a national treasure in Turkey. The Turkish Angora is a water baby that loves life on the go. Climbing, playing tricks, and dipping its paws in water are its favorite activities.

Fact file

» **Origin:** Turkey
» **Size:** Medium
» **Weight:** 6–12 lb (2.5–5.5 kg)
» **Color:** Mostly white, but can be a variety of colors
» **Character:** Affectionate, lively, energetic, and demanding

The Turkish Angora has large, slightly pointed ears.

Odd eyes

Turkish Angoras can have a range of eye colors, including blue, blue-green, and amber. Some cats of this breed sport a different color in each eye.

It has a graceful yet strong body.

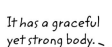

In the 1990s, the Ankara Zoo in Turkey saved this breed from extinction.

Nebelung

The Nebelung is a quiet and reserved cat, and loves keeping the same company and routine. It should be introduced to new people or changes at home gradually. This breed is affectionate and enjoys being a lap cat.

» **Origin:** United States
» **Size:** Medium
» **Weight:** 9–15 lb (4–7 kg)
» **Color:** Silver-blue
» **Character:** Gentle, loyal, sensitive, and clever

Epic origins

This breed's name was inspired by the title of a German epic poem called *Nibelungenlied*. The first two cats of the breed, Siegfried and Brunhilde, were named after characters in the poem.

The Nebelung's thick, silky fur needs regular brushing.

1921 cover of *Nibelungenlied*

The Nebelung looks like a long-haired version of the Russian Blue cat.

It has shorter fur on the lower legs.

This breed has a furry tail that is longer than its body.

Selkirk Rex

This sweet-natured cat wants a lot of love. Its dense but soft coat falls into curls or waves instead of neat lines. The Selkirk Rex can be either long-haired or short-haired.

» **Origin:** United States
» **Size:** Medium to large
» **Weight:** 10–18 lb (4.5–8 kg)
» **Color:** Variety of colors
» **Character:** Loving, patient, friendly, and relaxed

The Selkirk Rex has a round head and full cheeks.

The special, curled coat of this breed has given it the nickname "the cat in sheep's clothing."

The neck, stomach, and tail have the curliest fur.

Selkirk Mountains

This breed takes its name from the Selkirk Mountains of Canada and the United States. The first Selkirk Rex was a curly-haired kitten born in an animal shelter near these mountains.

Its thick tail has a rounded tip.

Tiffanie

The Tiffanie loves to communicate, be it chatting with its owner or protesting being left alone. This long-haired member of the Asian cat family always makes its voice heard. It is a gentle yet mischievous cat.

Fact file

» **Origin:** United Kingdom
» **Size:** Medium
» **Weight:** 9–14 lb (4–6.5 k
» **Color:** Variety of colors
» **Character:** Affectionate
  playful, clever, and
  demanding

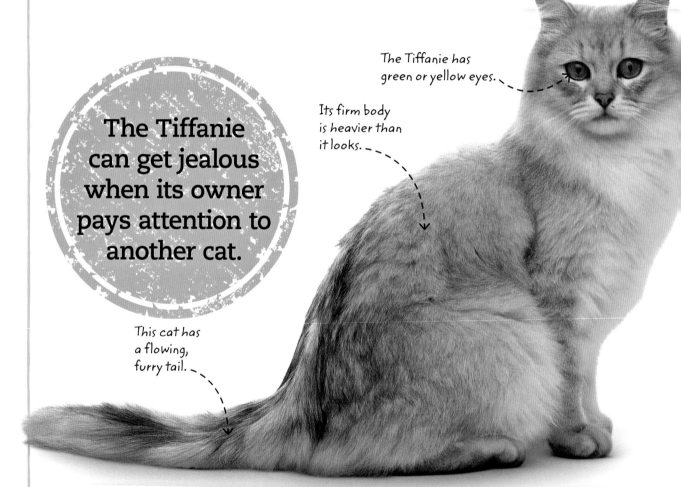

The Tiffanie has green or yellow eyes.

Its firm body is heavier than it looks.

The Tiffanie can get jealous when its owner pays attention to another cat.

This cat has a flowing, furry tail.

Burmese resemblance

The Tiffanie is a long-haired version of the Burmese cat. This breed originated from an unusual group of kittens born in London, United Kingdom, in 1981. These kittens had a Chinchilla Persian and a Lilac Burmese for parents.

Chantilly

The parents of the first Chantilly kittens were two long-haired, chocolate cats with golden eyes. The sweet-natured kittens looked just like their parents, and cats of this breed still look very similar today.

» **Origin:** United States
» **Size:** Medium
» **Weight:** 9–13 lb (4–6 kg)
» **Color:** Mostly chocolate brown, but can be a variety of colors
» **Character:** Gentle, calm, loyal, and affectionate

A Chantilly's happy chirp sounds a lot like a pigeon cooing.

Chocoholic's delight

Although the Chantilly can be a variety of colors, the original color of this breed was a deep chocolate brown. It's because of this coat color that the breed is called the "chocoholic's delight."

The Chantilly has glittering, golden eyes.

Its luxurious fur is soft to the touch.

This cat has a full, furry tail.

73

Scottish Fold

The first thing to notice about this breed from Scotland is its neatly folded ears. The Scottish Fold was discovered by a shepherd, who spotted an unusual kitten with folded ears in 1961.

Pop star favorite

American singer Taylor Swift is a proud owner of three felines. Two of them are Scottish Folds. They were featured in one of her music videos and go with her on tours.

Taylor Swift

American writer Peter Gethers's famous trilogy, Norton the Cat, is based on his adventures with his Scottish Fold, Norton.

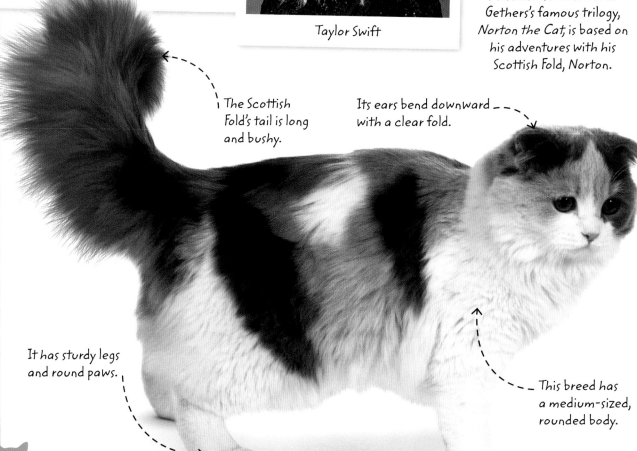

The Scottish Fold's tail is long and bushy.

Its ears bend downward with a clear fold.

It has sturdy legs and round paws.

This breed has a medium-sized, rounded body.

Manx

This breed usually has a missing tail, which has led people to make up stories about where it came from. While most cats use their tails for balance, the Manx is thought to have extra-sensitive inner ears to help it stay upright.

The Manx has a strong and sturdy body.

The tailless Manx can have no tail or a small stump.

The eyes are slightly angled toward its nose.

Both tailless and full-tailed Manx can be born in the same litter.

Its back legs are longer than the front legs.

The cabbit myth

According to a myth, long ago it was thought that the Manx was a cabbit—a mix between a cat and a rabbit. Its long back legs and short, stumpy tail led to this belief.

A sketch of the cabbit

Birman

The beautiful Birman is called the sacred cat of Burma (now Myanmar). This breed is said to have been created by a blue-eyed goddess, who blessed a temple cat by magically turning its yellow eyes blue.

The dark color on its face extends from its nose to its forehead.

Perfect partnership

German fashion designer Karl Lagerfeld had a Birman named Choupette. This cat modeled alongside him, and was also the inspiration for Lagerfeld's "Choupette" face handbags.

Karl Lagerfeld and Choupette

Its powerful body is longer than most long-haired cats.

The Birman has an evenly colored tail.

Birman kittens are born white, and get their dark patches as they grow.

Aphrodite Giant

This large feline, also called the Aphrodite or Cyprus cat, comes from the island of Cyprus. The Aphrodite Giant has long legs and enjoys climbing. It is a social cat, and gets along well with people as well as other pets.

» **Origin:** Cyprus
» **Size:** Large
» **Weight:** 10–18 lb (4.5–8 kg)
» **Color:** Variety of colors except pointed and mink
» **Character:** Gentle, social, loving, and active

The Aphrodite Giant has a triangular-shaped head.

Cats of St. Nicholas

Founded in the fourth century, the Holy Monastery of St. Nicholas of the Cats kept Aphrodite Giant cats to help control pests. It is said that the monastery had two bells—one for inviting people for prayer, and the other for calling the cats in for meals.

This breed is named after Aphrodite, the Greek goddess of beauty.

Monastery of St. Nicholas of the Cats

This breed has a full, bushy tail.

Mixed-breed cats

Mixed-breed cats are of no particular breed. Millions of them are kept as pets around the world, making them the most common domestic cats. They make great house cats and are known for being wonderful companions.

Félicette

A Parisian mixed-breed cat, named Félicette was the first and only cat to be successfully launched into space. She was trained alongside other cats by the French Space Agency, and her mission took place on October 18, 1963.

Cats being trained for spaceflight

The eyes of mixed-breed cats can be a range of colors.

Their fur can be any color or pattern.

These cats have strong and robust bodies with few health problems.

Hairless cats

While most cats are either long- or short-haired, there are some breeds that are hairless. It may look like they don't have any hair, but most of them have a fine layer of fur. Some ancient cats were hairless, but modern hairless cat breeds first appeared in the 1960s.

The Donskoy has large eyes compared to its small face.

Donskoy

This breed started with a hairless kitten found on the streets of Rostov-on-Don, in Russia. The gentle and friendly Donskoy can either be hairless, or have a partial coat on its body in a variety of colors.

It is medium to large in size.

This breed has long legs and thick paw pads.

Caring for a hairless cat

Looking after hairless cats requires special care and a lot of upkeep. Since these felines don't have thick fur like other cats, their skin is left mostly exposed. This lack of protection makes it very sensitive.

Keeping warm
In the fall and winter months, a hairless cat is likely to feel the cold more than other breeds. It is best to make sure that these cats are kept warm with cozy blankets.

Ukrainian Levkoy

The Ukrainian Levkoy breed has the Scottish Fold and the Donskoy as parents. These felines are curious, playful, and affectionate. They enjoy spending time with people, and get along well with children and other pets.

This unique cat has ears that fold inward.

The Ukrainian Levkoy's skin is covered with very fine hair.

Some Ukrainian Levkoy cats are born with straight ears.

Like most hairless cats, it has many wrinkles.

The long, narrow tail becomes thinner toward the tip.

Regular cleaning
A hairless cat's skin is very oily. This can lead to skin infections. These cats require weekly baths with a gentle shampoo to keep their skin healthy.

Staying inside
These cats have sensitive skin that can get sunburned easily. They should be kept indoors to protect them from harsh sunlight.

The cat family

Every cat in the world belongs to the same family of carnivores—the Felidae (fee-lee-day). This family is further divided into two groups, Pantherinae (pan-ther-ee-nay), which consists of big cats and Felinae (fee-lee-nay), which is split into seven subgroups of small cats.

Felinae (small cats)

This includes seven groups—ocelot, caracal, puma, small cat including domestic cats, lynx, leopard cat, and bay cat.

Felidae

Around forty different species of wildcats and domestic cats are included in this family.

Saber-toothed cat's skull

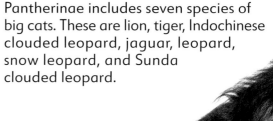

Pantherinae (big cats)

Pantherinae includes seven species of big cats. These are lion, tiger, Indochinese clouded leopard, jaguar, leopard, snow leopard, and Sunda clouded leopard.

Prehistoric cats

The cats of today shared an ancestor with the prehistoric saber-toothed cats, which are now extinct. Unlike the felines of today, the male and female saber-toothed cats were around the same size.

Male lions reach around 10 ft (3 m) in length, from the head to the base of the tail.

Ocelot group

This group includes the oncilla, Andean mountain cat, Geoffroy's cat, kodkod, margay, ocelot, pampas cat, and southern tiger cat.

Oncilla

Caracal

Caracal group

The caracal, African golden cat, and serval are all members of the caracal group.

Puma group

The cheetah, jaguarundi, and puma make up this small group of wildcats. The puma also has other names, such as cougar and mountain lion.

Cheetah

African wildcat

Small cat group

This group consists of the African wildcat, Chinese mountain cat, black-footed cat, European wildcat, jungle cat, and sand cat. The domestic cats we have as pets evolved from the African wildcat.

Eurasian lynx

Lynx group

The Eurasian lynx, Canadian lynx, bobcat, and Iberian lynx are part of the lynx group.

Cat characters

Think about how different people are from each other. They might be shy or outgoing, adventurous or careful. Cats are just the same, with a lot of different personalities.

For many cats, people are better to live with than other felines.

Long-haired cats are usually quieter than other felines.

Kitty cats

Kittens share many of the same personality traits as adult cats while growing up. If cat owners interact and play with their pets when they are still very young, the kittens will grow up to be more confident and friendly.

Friendly and playful
Kittens make a lot of noise. Games, such as hide-and-seek, show their playful streak.

Active and adventurous
Lively kittens love backyard games. They often find themselves at the center of all kinds of adventures.

Friendly or shy

A friendly cat is contented, and enjoys company and cuddling. It adjusts easily to new places and people. A quiet, shy cat, on the other hand, often prefers to be alone. It takes time to get comfortable with its owner as well as its new home.

A cat demanding food

Forceful

A strong spirit and pushy character help a forceful cat to get its own way. Often, a forceful cat will use its commanding and strong presence to get cuddles and snacks from its owner.

Curious

The curious and spontaneous cat is interested in absolutely everything. This cat likes exploring outside, climbing trees, playing games with humans or other cats, and welcomes all distractions!

A cat in a tree

Independent
When kittens are on the move, they often go exploring inside the house. They run, jump, and climb everywhere.

Sleepy
Kittens like to nap together after constantly being on the go. Once grown, they will sleep alone in warm, safe spots.

Hugging a cat can cause feel-good chemicals to be released in the brain.

Cat company

It is wonderful to have a furry pet around the house. But a cat is much more than that for its owner. A cat becomes a friend, proven to make people feel happier. The soothing vibrations of a cat's purr can make almost everyone feel more relaxed.

Cat therapy

Cats bring good vibes everywhere they go. This is the reason that sometimes they are taken to hospitals, homes for the elderly, and schools for children with disabilities. Petting these furry felines makes people feel better.

When people feel sad, it sometimes helps them to talk to a pet about what they're feeling. A cat will always be there to lend an ear.

Cats are so relaxing that owners may be less likely to suffer from heart attacks. High blood pressure can cause health problems, and petting cats can lower it.

Most cats are independent, but some enjoy being held and hugged.

Hunting habits

A domestic cat has similar hunting instincts to that of the other members of the cat family. Cats have all of the strength and skills needed for hunting. Unlike wildcats, pet cats are given their dinner, but they still like chasing birds and mice.

Mighty muscles

The powerful body of a cat is packed with muscles that enable it to make quick grabs. The strong back legs are used to make long leaps and high jumps. Its flexible body is designed to run at high speeds.

On the prowl

A cat's natural hunting instincts make it respond to anything that moves. This can be a bird in the yard or a motorized toy. The cat will follow its prey around quietly, keeping its body low to the ground as it gets ready to pounce.

Silent stalkers

Pet cats don't hunt to fill their stomachs, but for the thrill of the chase. They can sit quietly watching their prey for a long time before pouncing. Keep an eye on the fish tank! Cats can dip a paw in and try to hook out a fish.

Paws and claws

Cats' paws have thick, soft pads so they can move silently. Their claws are made of keratin, which is the same substance as in human fingernails.

Cats are marvelous movers. They walk on tiptoes, which helps them balance on narrow fences.

Cats can leap up to seven times their own height.

Cats may bring home prey to show off their hunting skills, or to give as a gift to their owners.

Cats use their sharp claws to grab prey or grip something for climbing.

Cats only bring out their claws when they are needed, and tuck them safely away when they are receiving cuddles.

Instinctive pounce

Pouncing comes very naturally to a cat. It is an instinctive behavior. Kittens start to pounce from the moment they begin to play.

All together

This book shows off some of the most popular domestic cat breeds in the world. While many of these felines have long, fluffy coats, some have short, thick fur, and the rest have no hair at all! Here you can see a selection of the cat breeds featured in this book.

European Shorthair
pg. 12

Chinese Li Hua
pg. 12

Ceylon
pg. 13

Khao Manee
pg. 13

American Wirehair
pg. 13

American Shorthair
pg. 14

British Shorthair
pg. 15

Korat
pg. 16

Bombay
pg. 17

Singapura
pg. 18

Abyssinian
pg. 19

Egyptian Mau
pg. 20

Ocicat
pg. 21

Australian Mist
pg. 22

Bengal
pg. 23

Chausie
pg. 28

Chartreux
pg. 29

Toyger
pg. 30

Serengeti
pg. 31

Siamese
pg. 32

Havana
pg. 33

American Burmese
pg. 34

European Burmese
pg. 35

Cornish Rex
pg. 36

Devon Rex
pg. 37

Pixiebob
pg. 40

Japanese Bobtail
pg. 41

Russian Blue
pg. 42

Snowshoe
pg. 43

Oriental
Shorthair
pg. 44

Tonkinese
pg. 45

British
Longhair
pg. 50

American
Bobtail
pg. 50

Ural Rex
pg. 51

Kurilian
Bobtail
pg. 51

Neva
Masquerade
pg. 51

Angora
pg. 52

Highlander
pg. 53

Ragdoll
pg. 54

Maine Coon
pg. 55

American
Curl
pg. 56

Persian
pg. 57

Himalayan
pg. 58

LaPerm
pg. 59

Norwegian
Forest Cat
pg. 60

Siberian
Forest Cat
pg. 61

Somali
pg. 62

Balinese
pg. 63

Turkish Van
pg. 68

Turkish Angora
pg. 69

Nebelung
pg. 70

Selkirk Rex
pg. 71

Tiffanie
pg. 72

Chantilly
pg. 73

Scottish Fold
pg. 74

Manx
pg. 75

Birman
pg. 76

Aphrodite
Giant
pg. 77

Donskoy
pg. 80

Ukrainian
Levkoy
pg. 81

Glossary

affectionate

warm and loving

allergy

bad reaction to fur or another substance, which usually brings on watery eyes and sneezing

ancestor

animal related to another, more recent animal

ancient

very old

big cat

large, wild member of the cat family, such as a lion or tiger

breed

type of animal with specific characteristics

breeder

person who arranges for kittens to be born with certain looks and personalities

carnivore

animal with biting teeth that eats meat

ceramic

clay heated at a very high temperature to make it hard

claws

sharp nails at the end of a paw or foot

companion

friend or someone you spend a lot of time with

domestic

animal that is cared for by people

epic

very long story or poem that takes place over a long period of time

extrovert

someone whose personality is lively, outgoing, and friendly

feline

cat, or something that is cat-like

flexible

something that bends without breaking

fur

soft hair that grows over most of a cat's body to keep it warm

glossy

smooth and shiny

grooming

brushing and cleaning fur, or cutting nails or hair

instinct

way of behaving, thinking, or feeling that comes naturally

keratin

substance found in a cat's claws and tongue as well as a human's skin and fingernails

kitten

young cat

litter

all the kittens that are born to a mother at the same time

litter box

container where cats can go to the bathroom

longhair

breed of cat with long, thick hair

monastery

building or a group of buildings in which monks (members of a religious community) live

muzzle

part of a cat's face that usually includes its nose and mouth

myth

popular story created to explain events, practices, and beliefs

pixie
imaginary, fairylike creature with pointed ears

plush
thick, soft, and velvety

pointed
pale fur with dark markings on the face, ears, nose, legs and tail

pounce
to jump on something

prehistoric
something that existed before information was written down

prey
animal that is killed by another animal for food

pupil
hole at the center of the eye that looks black and lets light in

robust
very strong or healthy

sacred
something holy, believed to have a connection with God

sense
animal's way of gathering information about its surroundings. The five main senses are smell, hearing, taste, sight, and touch

sensitive
capable of understanding other people's needs, problems, or feelings

shepherd
someone who takes care of sheep

shorthair
breed of cat with short hair or fur

sleek
smooth and glossy

slender
thin and graceful

speckled
covered with small spots and marks

spines
long, sharp points on all or part of an animal's body

spontaneous
something sudden

stocky
broad, solid, and sometimes short

streak
series of the same behavior, such as playfulness

sturdy
strong and firm

therapy
form of treatment designed to improve the well-being of people

tipping
different color at the tip of a cat's fur

tufted
area where thick hair grows together

upkeep
keeping something in good condition, such as fur

vibration
when something moves back and forth very quickly

vocabulary
group of words in a language, or all the words known to a person

wean
process by which young kittens are encouraged to feed on food other than their mother's milk

whiskers
stiff, sensitive hairs sprouting from a cat's face

wild
animal living free in the outside world

wrinkles
small lines or folds

Index

A

Abyssinian 7, 19, 62
adoption 6
adventure 84
African wildcats 83
age 9
American Bobtail 50
American Burmese 34
American Curl 56
American Shorthair 14
American Wirehair 13
anger 25, 26
Angora 52, 69
animal shelters 6
Aphrodite Giant 77
appetite 66
Australian Mist 7, 22

B

balance 5, 89
Balinese 63
baskets 64, 65
bathing 81
behavior 38–39
Bengal 23
big cats 82–83
birds 88
Birman 76
black cats 11
blue cats 11, 42
body features 4–5
body language 24–25
Bombay 17
bones 5
bowls, drinking 67
Brazilian Shorthair 6
British Longhair 50
British Shorthair 15
brushing 64, 65
Burmese 34–35, 45, 72

C

cabbits 75
caracals 83
care 64–65, 80–81
carnivores 66
carriers 64
cat family 82–83

cat flaps 65
Ceylon 13
Chantilly 73
characters 84–85
Chartreux 5, 29
Chausie 28
cheetahs 4, 83
Cheshire Cat 15
Chinese Li Hua 12
chocolate 67
chriping 27
claws 26, 89
climbing 48
collars 39
colors 10–11
commands 38, 39
communication 14, 24–25,
        26–27
Cornish Rex 36
curiosity 85
curled ears 53, 56
curly coats 36, 37, 59, 71

D

Devon Rex 37
diet 66
direction, sense of 48
distances, measuring 48
dollface 57
Donskoy 80
down 10
drinking 67
dry food 64, 66

E

ears 4, 8, 9, 48
Egyptian Mau 20
Egyptians, ancient 6, 20
emotional support cats 54
emotions 25
European Burmese 35
European Shorthair 7, 12
Exotics 46–47
extinction 69, 82
eye color 8, 42, 43, 46,
        69, 76
eyes 4, 8, 9, 49

FG

fear 25
Felidae 82
Felinae 82
fish 67
folded ears 74, 81
food 8, 64, 65, 66–67
foot pads 4, 5, 89
forcefulness 85
fresh food 66, 67
friendliness 85
fur 10–11
grooming 64, 65
growling 26

H

hair 10
hairless cats 11, 80–81
happiness 25, 27
harnesses 39
Havana 33
hearing 4, 8, 9, 48
Highlander 53
Himalayan 58
hissing 26, 39
hunting 5, 88–89

IJK

independence 38, 85, 87
Japanese Bobtail 7, 41
jumping 88, 89
keratin 67, 89
Khao Manee 13

kittens 8–9, 27, 66, 84–85
Korat 16
Kurilian Bobtail 51

L

La Perm 59
learning 9
leashes 38, 39
lions 4, 82
litter boxes 65
litters 8
locks 28
long-haired exotics 47
long-haired cats 11, 47, 50–51, 52–63, 68–77, 84
lynx 83

MN

Maine Coon 4, 55
Maneki-neko (beckoning cat) 41
Manx 75
markings 10–11
meat 66, 67
meowing 26, 27, 38, 41
mice 61, 77, 88
milk 8, 66, 67
mixed-breed cats 78–79
mood 25, 26
muscles 88
muzzles 33
myths and legends 32, 70, 75
Nebelung 70
Neva Masquerade 51
nighttime 48, 49
Norwegian Forest Cat 60
nose 4

OP

ocelots 21, 83
Ocicat 21
oncillas 83
orange cats 10
Oriental Longhair 52
Oriental Shorthair 44
Pantherinae 82
papillae 67
paws 4, 39, 89
Persian 57
personality 47, 84–85
petting 25
Pixiebob 40
play 9, 65, 84, 89
pointed cats 11, 32, 43, 63

pouncing 88, 89
prehistoric cats 82
prey 88, 89
prowling 88
pumas 83
pupils 4, 49
purring 27, 86

RS

Ragdoll 54
Romans 6
routine 65
Russian Blue 42
saber-toothed cats 82
scent marking 5, 25, 26
Scottish Fold 74
scratching 26, 65
scratching posts 65
Selkirk Rex 71
senses 4, 48–49
sepia agouti 18
Serengeti 31
servals 31
short-haired cats 11, 12–13, 14–23, 28–37, 40–47, 71
shyness 85
Siamese 32, 45, 63
Siberian Forest Cat 61
sight 4, 8, 9, 49
Singapura 5, 18
sit command 39
size 4–5
skeletons 5
skin 80, 81
skulls 5
sleep 4, 65, 85
smell, sense of 4, 49
smoke patterns 44
Snow Marbled Bengal 23
Snowshoe 6, 43
Somali 62
spaceflight 78
stalking 88
sunburn 81
Swift, Taylor 74
swimming 68

T

tabby cats 10
tailless cats 75
tails 5, 25
talking 26–27
taste, sense of 49
teeth 5, 66
territory 5, 26

therapy 87
Tiffanie 72
toes 40
toileting 65
tongues 67
Tonkinese 45
topcoats 10
tortoiseshell cats 11
touch 4, 48
Toyger 30
toys 65, 88
training 38–39
transport 64
treats 38, 39
tricks 38–39
Turkish Angora 69
Turkish Van 68

UV

Ukrainian Levkoy 81
undercoats 10
Ural Rex 51
vibrations 48
Vikings 60

WY

warmth 80
water 64, 65, 66, 67
waving paws 39
weight, monitoring 34
wet food 64, 66
whiskers 4, 48
white cats 10
wildcats 4, 21, 31, 82–83
winter coats 62
yowling 27

Acknowledgments

Dorling Kindersley would like to thank the following people for their assistance in the preparation of this book: Agey George, Olivia Stanford, Marie Greenwood, and Rona Skene for editorial support; Polly Goodman for proofreading; and Helen Peters for the index.

The publisher would like to thank the following for their kind permission to reproduce their photographs:

(Key: a-above; b-below/bottom; c-center; f-far; l-left; r-right; t-top)

1–96 Dreamstime.com: Nadezhda Bolotina. **1 Dreamstime. com:** Vladyslav Starozhylov (b). **2 Dreamstime.com:** 9dreamstudio (tc); Gurinaleksandr (bc). **3 Dreamstime. com:** Oksun70 (br); Sergioua (cra). **4–5 Alamy Stock Photo:** Juniors Bildarchiv RF / F237 (t). **4 Dreamstime.com:** Kucher Serhii (br). **5 Dreamstime.com:** Krissi Lundgren (br); Kucher Serhii (bl). **6 Dreamstime.com:** Isselee (crb); Nevodka (cl). **Getty Images / iStock:** Thinkstock / Stockbyte (bl). **7 Dreamstime.com:** Isselee (tc); Troichenko (bc). **Getty Images / iStock:** fuiyau yap (tr). **naturepl.com:** Robert Pickett (cr). **9 Dreamstime.com:** Ruth Black (tr); Oksun70 (br). **10 Dreamstime.com:** Michael Przekop / Przekopm (bl). **11 Alamy Stock Photo:** Animal Photography (bl). **Dreamstime.com:** Adogslifephoto (bc/Longhair); Isselee (bc); Stanislav Tolubaev (br). **Shutterstock.com:** OksanaSusoeva (cr). **12 Dreamstime.com:** Isselee (tr). **Getty Images / iStock:** Juliano703 (bl). **13 Alamy Stock Photo:** Juniors Bildarchiv / F215 (tr). **Dreamstime.com:** Sheila Fitzgerald (cl). **naturepl.com:** Yves Lanceau (br). **14 Depositphotos Inc:** lufimorgan (bc). **Dreamstime.com:** Aleksandr Volchanskiy (c). **15 Dreamstime.com:** Isselee (bl). **Getty Images / iStock:** Duncan1890 (crb). **16 Getty Images / iStock:** Nnikiss (cl). **17 Dreamstime. com:** Alexandrebes (cr); Vladimir Grekov (br). **18 Dreamstime. com:** Nynke Van Holten (c); Krissi Lundgren (br). **19 Alamy Stock Photo:** The History Collection (br). **Dreamstime. com:** Slowmotiongli (cra); Troichenko (tc). **20 Alamy Stock Photo:** Animal Photography (l); Charles Walker Collection (br). **21 Dreamstime.com:** Kucher Serhii (b). **Shutterstock. com:** L–N (c). **22 Dreamstime.com:** Andrii Tokarchuk (br). **naturepl.com:** Robert Pickett (c). **23 Dreamstime.com:** Erik Lam (l). **Getty Images / iStock:** andreaskrappweis (br). **24–25 Getty Images:** Nick David. **25 Dreamstime.com:** Kucher Serhii (cr); Sonsedskaya (cra). **Getty Images / iStock:** seraficus (br). **26 Dreamstime.com:** Adogslifephoto (c); Zanna Peshnina (cl); Mimnr1 (tr). **27 Dorling Kindersley:** Pat Cherry (tr). **Dreamstime.com:** Oriol Prat (br); Thawats (cla); Anastasiia Prokofyeva (bc). **Getty Images / iStock:** Voren1 (cr). **28 Dreamstime.com:** Taniawild (c); Oleksandra Troian (br). **29 Dreamstime.com:** Kucher Serhii (c). **Getty Images:** Manuel Freres / Stringer (bc). **30 Dreamstime.com:** Natalyka (c). **Shutterstock. com:** Roe Ethridge / The LIFE Picture Collection (crb). **31 Dreamstime.com:** Kucher Serhii (b). **32 Dreamstime. com:** Diomidov (cl); Golden Shark (br). **33 Shutterstock. com:** Jolanta Jd (br). **34 Dreamstime.com:** Kostiantyn Voitenko (cl). **Shutterstock.com:** IrinaFoto (b). **35 Dreamstime. com:** Slowmotiongli (c). **36 Dreamstime.com:** Nynke Van Holten (c); Tommason (cra); Anna Utekhina (crb). **37 Dreamstime.com:** Ian Woolcock (br); Vladyslav Starozhylov (c). **38–39 Alamy Stock Photo:** Giel, O. / juniors@wildlife. **38 Dreamstime.com:** Maria Ivanova (bc). **39 Alamy Stock Photo:** Erich Schmidt / imageBROKER (bl). **Dreamstime.com:** Vladimir Polikarpov (crb). **Getty Images:** Peter Dazeley / The Image Bank (fcrb). **41 Dreamstime.com:** Chaoss (cr). **Getty Images / iStock:** fuiyau yap (cra). **42 Alamy Stock Photo:** The Art Collector / Heritage–Images / The Print Collector (clb). **Dreamstime. com:** Tanijana (br). **Shutterstock.com:** Kirill Vorobyev (c). **43 Dreamstime.com:** Axel Bueckert (cl); Nynke Van Holten (c). **Getty Images:** Bruce Glikas / FilmMagic (crb). **44 Getty Images:** Agency Animal Picture / Photodisc (c). **45 Alamy Stock Photo:** petographer (l). **Getty Images / iStock:**

ahloch (cr). **46–47 Alamy Stock Photo:** Chanita Chokchaikul / EyeEm (cr). **47 Depositphotos Inc:** ewastudio (crb). **Dreamstime.com:** Cynoclub (cra). **Shutterstock.com:** Pherawit Rattanachot (bc). **48 Depositphotos Inc:** Lindasj2 (crb). **Dreamstime.com:** Ahavelaar (clb). **49 123RF.com:** Miroslav Beneda (tl); David Carillet (cla). **Alamy Stock Photo:** Paul.Biggins (clb); The Picture Art Collection (cra). **Dreamstime.com:** Elena Pyatkova (crb). **50 Dreamstime. com:** Isselee (tr); Ievgeniia Miroshnichenko (bc). **51 Alamy Stock Photo:** sylvia born (c); Tierfotoagentur / R. Richter (tc). **Dreamstime.com:** Nynke Van Holten (bl). **52 Alamy Stock Photo:** The Picture Art Collection (bl). **53 Alamy Stock Photo:** Idamini (c); Tierfotoagentur / H. Bollich (br). **Dreamstime.com:** Holly Kuchera (bl). **54 Dreamstime. com:** Tatyana Vychegzhanina (br). **55 Alamy Stock Photo:** © Fine Art Images / Heritage Images (cra). **Dreamstime. com:** Isselee (l). **56 Dreamstime.com:** Isselee (c). **Shutterstock.com:** Jeanette Virginia Goh (clb). **57 Dreamstime.com:** Mustafa Ferhat Beksen (cla); Isselee (b). **58 Alamy Stock Photo:** Trinity Mirror / Mirrorpix (bc). **Dreamstime.com:** Olena Danileiko (tl). **59 Dreamstime. com:** Nils Jacobi (cra). **60 Alamy Stock Photo:** INTERFOTO / History (cra). **61 Alamy Stock Photo:** Tierfotoagentur / R. Richter (c). **Dreamstime.com:** Pisotckii (bc). **62 Getty Images:** Lisa Beattie (clb). **63 Dreamstime.com:** Paulus Rusyanto (c). **64 Dreamstime.com:** 9dreamstudio (cr); Jevtic (tl); Illia Bondar (crb). **65 Dreamstime.com:** Bagwold (fbl); Alena Ozerova (cla); Pimmimemom (bl); Famveldman (crb). **66 Alamy Stock Photo:** Giel, O. / juniors@wildlife / Juniors Bildarchiv GmbH (tr). **Dreamstime.com:** Natalyka (br); Sergioua (c); Okssi68 (bl). **67 Alamy Stock Photo:** Juniors Bildarchiv / F193 (cl). **Dreamstime.com:** Arsenii Popel (br). **68 Alamy Stock Photo:** Animal Photography (br). **69 Dreamstime.com:** Leoniek6 (br). **Shutterstock. com:** AyhanTuranMenekay (cl). **70 Alamy Stock Photo:** Zuri Swimmer (c). **Dreamstime.com:** Katrina Trninich (bl); Kirill Vorobyev (crb). **71 Dreamstime.com:** Jaahnlieb (crb); Dmitri Pravdjukov (b). **72 Dreamstime.com:** Lavigna (br). **73 Srijani Ganguly:** (cr). **74 Alamy Stock Photo:** Ben Birchall / PA Images (c). **75 messybeast.com:** (br). **76 Alamy Stock Photo:** Fashion illustrations (cr). **Dreamstime.com:** Cynoclub (br); Isselee (b). **77 Alamy Stock Photo:** Ioannis Toutoungi (br). **Dreamstime.com:** Felis (clb). **78 Getty Images:** Keystone (clb). **78–79 Dreamstime.com:** Nikolay Petkov. **80 Alamy Stock Photo:** PLANCHARD Eric / hemis.fr (c). **SuperStock:** Jean–Michel Labat / Mary Evans Picture Library (bc). **81 Alamy Stock Photo:** Zoonar / Petr Malyshev (bl). **Dreamstime.com:** Olgavolodina (crb); Pavlo Vakhrushev (cl). **82 Dreamstime. com:** Rimpilstilskin (cl, br). **83 Alamy Stock Photo:** Ann and Steve Toon (crb). **Dreamstime.com:** Isselee (cl, bl). **Shutterstock.com:** Eric Isselee (tc). **84–85 Dreamstime. com:** Oksun70. **84 123RF.com:** andreykuzmin (crb). **Getty Images / iStock:** cynoclub (cb). **85 Dreamstime.com:** Gurinaleksandr (br); Thorsten Nilson (tc); Bidouze Stphane (cr); Oksun70 (clb). **86–87 Getty Images:** Don Mason. **87 Getty Images / iStock:** Maximastudio (cra); Kemal Yildirim (crb). **88 123RF.com:** bloodua (br). **88–89 Alamy Stock Photo:** blickwinkel / H. Schmidbauer (c). **Dreamstime.com:** Piolka (t). **89 Dreamstime.com:** Chernetskaya (clb); Konstanttin (tl); Jagodka (c); Kristo Robert (cra). **Fotolia:** Eric Isselee (cb). **Getty Images / iStock:** Nitiphonphat (bc). **Shutterstock.com:** Elena Rozhenok (cr). **90 Alamy Stock Photo:** Animal Photography (c/Egyptian Mau); Juniors Bildarchiv / F215 (cra). **Dreamstime.com:** Sheila Fitzgerald (ca/white cat); Isselee (fcla, fcra); Aleksandr Volchanskiy (ca); Nynke Van Holten (c, bc); Troichenko (c/abyssinian cat); Kucher Serhii (cr, cb,

cb/Serengeti); Erik Lam (fclb); Taniawild (clb); Natalyka (cb/toyger); Vladyslav Starozhylov (bc/Devon Rex). **Getty Images / iStock:** Juliano703 (cla); fuiyau yap (br). **naturepl.com:** Yves Lanceau (ca/American wirehair); Robert Pickett (fcr). **Shutterstock.com:** IrinaFoto (fbl); Kirill Vorobyev (fbr). **91 Alamy Stock Photo:** Animal Photography (fclb); petographer (tc); Tierfotoagentur / R. Richter (tr, c); sylvia born (ftr); Idamini (ca); Ioannis Toutoungi (bc/Cyprus); PLANCHARD Eric / hemis.fr (br). **Dreamstime.com:** Nynke Van Holten (ftl, fcla); Isselee (tc/British longhair, ca/Maine coon, cra, fcra, bc); Ievgeniia Miroshnichenko (tc/American bobtail); Leoniek6 (clb); Katrina Trninich (cb); Dmitri Pravdjukov (cb/Selkirk rex); Pavlo Vakhrushev (fbr). **Getty Images:** Agency Animal Picture / Photodisc (tr). **Dreamstime. com:** Ahavelaar (bl); Oksun70 (br). **93 Depositphotos Inc:** ewastudio (br). **94 Dreamstime.com:** Okssi68 (tc); Anastasiia Prokofyeva (tr); Alena Ozerova (br). **95 Dreamstime. com:** Thawats (cr). **96 Dreamstime. com:** Oksun70 (br)

Cover images: Front: Alamy Stock Photo: Animal Photography cr; **Dreamstime.com:** Isselee cl, br; **Fotolia:** Roman Milert ca; **Shutterstock.com:** OksanaSusoeva tr; **Back: Alamy Stock Photo:** Animal Photography cl, Juniors Bildarchiv RF / F237 ftl, Tierfotoagentur / R. Richter cb; **Dreamstime.com:** 9dreamstudio fcra, Bagwold fbl, Isselee cla, Nevodka tr, Oksun70 tl, clb/ (kittens playing), Kucher Serhii crb, br, Troichenko cr; **Getty Images / iStock:** Voren1 clb; **Spine: 123RF.com:** Dima Sobko t; **Dreamstime.com:** Bagwold cb.

All other images © Dorling Kindersley